W9-DCH-624

The First Christian Theology

Studies in Romans

The First Christian Theology
Studies in Romans

Herman A. Hoyt

BMH Books
Winona Lake, IN 46590

Copyright 1977 by
Baker Book House Company
ISBN: 0-88469-038-5
Printed in the United States of America

Co-published by
Baker Book House
Grand Rapids, Michigan
and
BMH Books
Winona Lake, Indiana

To
My Firstborn Son
JOSEPH PAUL
Who Was
Named for the Great
Apostle

Acknowledgments

In addition to the many books that are listed in the documentation and the bibliography, lectures in Bible classes in college and seminary, sermons on various texts, and observations overheard in the course of Christian experience were helpful in writing this monograph. Studies in the Greek language, which provided a channel to the original text, and studies in the field of theology, which provided insight into the doctrine of the epistle, are not among the least of these.

Those who have typed the manuscript and with great care have proofread the entire production include Miss Judy Vulgamore; Mrs. Betty Vulgamore, assistant to the secretary to the president of Grace Schools, and Mrs. Agnes N. Derr, secretary to the president. In addition to checking mechanical details, valuable suggestions were made as to wording, arrangement, and expression.

The editor of the Brethren Missionary Herald Company, the Reverend Charles Turner, provided the opportunity to study and prepare these studies in the Book of Romans, making the arrangements for this book to be published jointly by Baker Book House of Grand Rapids, Michigan, and the Brethren Missionary Herald Company of Winona Lake, Indiana.

Review of and further research in this epistle have resulted in inestimable blessing as the veil upon old truth was drawn aside and new vistas of truth burst forth. May all those who study the Epistle to the Romans with this monograph as a guide be ushered into new realms of blessing, assurance, and certainty of that salvation in Christ Jesus our Lord.

Herman A. Hoyt
Winona Lake, Indiana
May 1, 1975

Contents

Introduction to the Epistle to the Romans

5-15-77

William Tyndale, in his prologue to the Epistle to the Romans in the 1534 edition of his English New Testament, wrote these words at its beginning:

> Forasmuch as this epistle is the principal and most excellent part of the New Testament, and most pure *Euangelion*, that is to say glad tidings and that we call gospel, and also a light and a way in unto the whole scripture, I think it meet that every Christian man not only know it by rote and without the book, but also exercise himself therein evermore continually, as with the daily bread of the soul. No man verily can read it too oft or study it too well: for the more it is studied the easier it is, the more it is chewed the pleasanter it is, and the more groundly it is searched the preciouser things are found in it, so great treasure of spiritual things lieth hid therein.

Martin Luther, one of the leaders of the Reformation, added his commendation: "It is the chief part of the New Testament and the perfect gospel." The poet Coleridge paid it high tribute when he said that it is "the most profound work in existence." And no less a commentator than Godet declared it to be "the cathedral of the Christian faith."

A. The author of this epistle is the apostle Paul. He places his name at the very outset of the epistle (1:1) and the remainder of the epistle confirms this claim. In general, scholarship has agreed. So universally is Paul acclaimed the author that it is unnecessary to make any formal proof here. Vocabulary, theological argument, logic, passion, movement, and the grand theme of the epistle point to none other than the greatest of the apostles. From the opening word to the closing "Amen," this man's life and experience, passion and purpose, mental acumen and spiritual dynamic provide the atmosphere and pervade the sanctity of the entire book. Even though the authorship of the Epistle to the Romans is beyond dispute, the reader must not fail to appreciate the significance of the author in relation to the content of the epistle.

Paul was born in the city of Tarsus (Acts 22:3), the capital city of the Roman province of Cilicia, located about seven hundred miles north of Jerusalem. This fact also made him a Roman citizen (Acts 22:25-28). Though his birth date is unknown, it was probably not far from that of Christ. The very fact that he is referred to as a young man at the time of the stoning of Stephen would indicate that he is probably not far from thirty (Acts 7:58).

Tarsus was "no mean city" (Acts 21:39). In the ancient world it ranked with Athens and Alexandria for culture and learning. In addition to being one of the three university centers of that day, it was characterized by moral corruption. In this city Paul had access to Greek and Roman learning, a fact evidenced by his acquaintance with Greek philosophy and Roman law. In addition to this training, he was given the privilege to sit at the feet of one of the greatest of the ancient Hebrew teachers, Gamaliel, in the city of Jerusalem (Acts 22:3).

Paul was in every sense a Jew. He was "circumcised the eighth day, of the stock of Israel, of the tribe of Benjamin, an Hebrew of the Hebrews; as touching the law, a Pharisee; concerning zeal, persecuting the church; touching the righteousness which is in the law, blameless" (Phil. 3:5-6). His father before him was also a Pharisee, and there is some reason to believe that he was rather well-to-do, and this may explain what Paul meant when he asserted that at conversion he lost everything (Phil. 3:7-8). It may have been in his father's employ that he learned the art of weaving tent cloth (Acts 18:2-3).

All this qualified Paul for the position to which he early attained, membership in the Sanhedrin of Israel (Acts 6:12; 7:58; 8:1). To belong to this august body in Israel one had to be at least thirty years of age. The persuasion, passion, and persistence of this man, a Pharisee, made him the likely candidate to lead the Sadducean persecution against the church (Acts 7:58—8:1). It was on one of these arduous journeys to apprehend followers of Christ that Paul was taken captive by Christ and inducted into the ministry (Acts 9:1-20). The immediate revelation of God to Paul on the Damascus road and the postgraduate course in the desert (Gal. 1:16-17) prepared Paul for more than thirty years of ministry and the writing of the greatest epistle in the New Testament.

In studying this epistle it is important above all things to avoid the peril of "modernizing Paul."[1] In the theological climate of our day, there is a temptation to tone down the uncongenial or sharp and caustic reasoning of the apostle. Unconsciously the student of this epistle may seek to modify the concepts of the apostle in an attempt to bring them into a closer conformity with current thinking. This is to do violence to the meaning and message of the man. He must be allowed to be himself and speak the message God gave to him.

B. The people to whom Paul addressed this epistle were the saints that were in Rome (1:7). All the available facts suggest that this church was no recent development. The historical note in Acts in reference to those in attendance at the feast of Pentecost names ". . . strangers of Rome, Jews and Proselytes" (Acts 2:10). This is the only European contingent named, and this could explain the origin of the Roman church. They heard Peter preach at the feast of Pentecost, and some of them were saved and returned to start the church.

History makes clear that there was a Jewish community in Rome as early as the second century B.C. Faithful to the commands of the Old Testament law, some pilgrims made the long journey to Jerusalem to observe the various feasts, among which was the feast of Pentecost. In the good providence of God they experienced the miracles of Pentecost at the outpouring of the Spirit, heard the message of Peter, and were added to the church. When the feast was over they returned to their homes in Rome and organized the church of that city. By the time Paul wrote to them their faith had been so amply demonstrated that it was spoken of throughout the whole world (Rom. 1:8).

---

1. F. F. Bruce, *The Epistle of Paul to the Romans* (Grand Rapids: Wm. B. Eerdmans Publishing Co., 1969), p. 10.

No apostle was directly responsible for the origin of the church in Rome. This excludes Peter from the realm of possibility. Peter was still in Jerusalem at the time of the Jerusalem Council (A.D. 50), and the church was in existence before this. The Emperor Claudius banished Jews from Rome in A.D. 49, an edict which caught Priscilla and Aquila. When they arrived in Corinth (Acts 18:2-3), they were already Christians, which argues for the existence of the church in Rome long before A.D. 49. Even though there is strong reason to believe that Peter and Paul were both martyred there, we know that neither of them had any part in establishing the church.

Even though the constituency of the membership consisted of Jews and Gentiles, it seems clear that the original group of believers consisted "entirely of Jewish Christians."[2] An expulsion order from the emperor sent Jewish Christians fleeing from Rome. But by that time a considerable number of Gentiles had joined the Christian community; and even though the Jews later returned, by this time Gentiles far outnumbered Jews. Certain references in the Book of Romans can be explained no other way except to recognize a predominantly Gentile membership (1:5-6, 12-14; 6:19; 11:13, 28-31).

C. The place and date of the writing of this epistle are fairly certain. The key to the dating of its writing clusters about the collection for the poor saints at Jerusalem (I Cor. 16:1-3). In addition to the instructions to the churches given in I Corinthians, there are further instructions given in II Corinthians 8 and 9. By the time the apostle is ready to carry this contribution to Jerusalem he is just completing the writing of the Epistle to the Romans (15:25-27).

It becomes apparent from these facts that Romans was written after II Corinthians. I Corinthians was written from Ephesus during Paul's three-year ministry there. II Corinthians was written, probably from Philippi in Macedonia, shortly thereafter. When Paul had finally arrived in Corinth the second time for a

2. Bruce, p. 15.

three-months' stay (Acts 20:1-3), it was doubtless from there that he wrote the Epistle to the Romans and charged Phoebe (Rom. 16:1), a resident of Cenchrea, to carry the epistle to Rome (see subscription, KJV). Cenchrea was the seaport of Corinth, perhaps three miles distant, and Phoebe was intending to make the journey to Rome.

The date for the epistle becomes a valid inference. It must have been late A.D. 56, or early A.D. 57. The journey by land through Macedonia to Syria and from there to Jerusalem grew out of the plot of Jews to kill him. The time consumed by that journey, together with the two years in prison in Caesarea (Acts 24:27) and the long journey across the Mediterranean by ship to Rome, may well have consumed three years (Acts 27-28), so that Paul arrived for the first time in Rome about A.D. 60. Believers in Rome would have had three years of time in which to read and digest the message of his epistle before his coming. And when he finally arrived some of the brethren in Christ came out to Appii Forum to meet him (Acts 28:15).

D. There are problems that gather about this epistle, but they are in no sense insuperable. These problems have developed because of the scanty information available on the one hand, and confusing information on the other. Some manuscripts omit the words "in Rome" in verses 7 and 15 of chapter 1. The benediction of 16:20 (KJV) varies in position. Some manuscripts locate it at verse 24, and still others at the end of the chapter. The doxology recorded in 16:25-27 is also variously located in the manuscripts. Some place it at the end of chapter 14, some at the end of chapter 15, and still others at the end of chapter 16.

Perhaps more serious is the shorter recension of the epistle. One ancient writer declares that Marcion the heretic either cut away or separated the last two chapters from the preceding portion of the epistle. Several of the Church Fathers made no use of the last two chapters of the epistle, suggesting that they must have had a text in their hands which did not contain these chapters. Surely Tertullian, Irenaeus, and Cyprian would have used material contained therein if it had been available to them.

The great Latin manuscript Amiatinus as well as other Latin manuscripts omit these chapters. But in the face of the majority of manuscripts that carry these chapters there is nothing conclusive about their absence in the few.

Many scholars have puzzled over the fact that chapter 16 carries a whole list of names. To them it has seemed that perhaps this chapter was never intended for Rome, but rather had Ephesus as its destination. This is based on the conclusion that Paul could not have so many friends in a church where he had never ministered. The familiarity of Paul with these people and their labors could be true if this chapter had been directed to Ephesus, but it would be entirely unnatural if intended for Rome. However, all this theorizing is based on insufficient information. As a matter of fact, almost every assumption concerning Ephesian destination as opposed to Roman destination can be met with valid refutation.

It is therefore far more reasonable to take the epistle in its entirety as it stands in the common versions of today. From the standpoint of its message, the argument moves smoothly and logically from its opening words to its final conclusion.

E. The occasion for the writing of this epistle is another matter of concern. What prompted the apostle to write this epistle? For years he had cherished the desire to go to Rome (Acts 19:21). This fits in with the missionary principles of Paul. He did not despise small places, but he did desire to reach the centers of population and establish bases of operation. So his travels had taken him to all the great cities of the East. There was just one great center of population that had eluded him up to this point—Rome, the largest city in the empire. Antioch, the empire's second city in size, had been his original base of operation. Corinth was the third city in size. He had been there. Ephesus was the fourth in size, and he had been there.

God was not yet through with him in the East, so that is why all his plans had gone astray (Rom. 1:13). But now that the work is finished, it would appear as viewed by the apostle; and Paul lays plans to pass through Rome on his way to Spain and the West

(Rom. 15:18-24). There is one duty he must yet perform, and that is the delivery of the gifts collected in the churches for the poor saints in Jerusalem (Rom. 15:25-28). His lifelong ambition is now on the verge of realization. Phoebe's trip to the great city provides the necessary spark to write this letter and prepare the way for his coming.

His heart warms to the vision of ministry in the city of Rome (Rom. 1:8-12). He has many friends in Rome known to him, as witness the list in the final chapter. He remembers them by name before the throne of grace. It would be his great delight to impart to them some spiritual gift (1:11)—not in the sense of starting a church, for his ambition has been missionary, to reach the un-evangelized millions, not to build on another man's foundation (15:20). But with the worldwide vision in his heart (1:13-16), he could, at least at the moment, realize his supreme ambition to meet the universal need of mankind with the knowledge of an all-sufficient gospel by unfolding in this letter to them the vast reaches of God's provision for lost humanity.

F. The purpose for the writing of this epistle grows out of the occasion, though perhaps it extends far beyond that. Many suggestions have been made, and many of them are far afield.[3] Surely Paul was not aiming at Jewish Christianity, nor attempting to conciliate Jews and Gentiles. He could not have had in mind a mere summing up of his own experiences. But a fivefold purpose is discernible.

1. *It was official in that he sought to bridge the gulf between himself and the church in Rome.* That is probably the import of the first seven verses of the epistle. He is an apostle especially set aside for ministry among the Gentiles (Gal. 2:8). The Roman church is the only church among the Gentiles for which he has not been immediately used, or instrumental, in bringing into existence. The revelation committed to him was uniquely designed for Gentiles, and it was his business to get it to them.

3. Donald Guthrie, *New Testament Introduction: The Pauline Epistles* (Chicago: Inter-Varsity Press, 1964), pp. 25-28.

Though he had many friends in that church, without doubt, the vast number of Gentiles in it deserved the help he could give and he must establish a relation. The letter provided the immediate instrument for accomplishing this relation.

2. *It was personal in that he sought to reach them on a common level.* In some sense verses 8-15 are intended to accomplish this end. His commendation of their faith (v. 8), his prayer for them by name (v. 9), and his petition to visit them (v. 10) would most certainly warm their hearts and create in them a feeling of anticipation and expectancy. Many of them he already knew from former experience, and this would be sure to set them thinking about the good times of the past and put them to talking to the others of what it means to fellowship with Paul.

3. *It was spiritual in that by means of the letter, as well as by arriving in their midst, there might be a wholesome impartation to them* (v. 11). A spiritual message in a letter will result in establishing in the faith, just as word of mouth in their presence. When he arrives on the scene there will be a requital in kind for him. Their faith will bring mutual benefit to him. In fact, the study of this epistle will so refresh their spirits and kindle their thoughts that they will be overflowing with expressions of delight for the new visions of truth that have come to them.

4. *It was evangelical in its purpose, for he expected to harvest some fruit as a result.* This was his purpose and experience among other Gentiles, even by letter; and it is altogether reasonable to expect that he had this in mind when writing this letter (v. 13). The word will not return void. How wonderful it would be to witness growth in grace, growth in numbers, and perhaps even find some among them ready to answer the call to missionary endeavor, maybe even accompany him in his mission into Spain (15:24, 28).

5. *It was theological in that he sought to resolve the problems with which Gentile converts were confronted.* Surely the apostle does not mean that his desire to preach the gospel is to be limited

to a few sentences that constitute the core of this great message (1:14-17). That is certainly not the case if the remainder of this epistle is any indication of what he has in mind by verses 16 and 17.

By this time, the apostle has been in the ministry of Christ for more than twenty years. He has been in every great center of the Roman Empire except Rome. Beginning in Tarsus and marking the course of his ministry he has confronted all the great thinkers, Jewish and Gentile. He has confronted the problems troubling the minds of people. He has come to realize that there must be some effort made to integrate the Christian faith with the facts of reality and resolve the problems facing Christians.

As a result, this epistle takes on the form of a theological treatise. It runs the gamut of truth from Genesis to Revelation and deals with matters touching on everything from creation to the consummation. As such, it is the only theological treatise in the Bible covering the entire scope of reality. Though it does not enlarge on the doctrine of the church and eschatology, it cannot be said that it does not touch on these, especially in chapters 8-11. The full effect of this message cannot help but bring the reader into worshipful prostration before the God of all grace.

G. The influence of this epistle on the hearts of men has been phenomenal. The greatness of this epistle has captured the greatest minds in history. This greatness has been exhibited "in the importance of its subject matter, the comprehensiveness of its grasp, the acuteness of its reasoning, the breadth of its outlook, and the vigor of its style."[4] Such men as Augustine, Luther, Wesley, and Barth were moved by this message and launched far-reaching movements as a result.

Augustine was a great theologian of the early church. He was a native of North Africa, and at the time of coming to grips with the message of Romans, was a professor of rhetoric at Milan in Italy. He sat weeping in the garden of a friend, almost persuaded

4. Henry Clarence Thiessen, *Introduction to the New Testament* (Grand Rapids: Wm. B. Eerdmans Publishing Co., 1943), p. 219.

to begin a new life, yet lacking the final stint of courage to break with the old. From a neighboring house a child's voice reached his ears, "*Tolle, lege! Tolle, lege!*," meaning to him, "Take up and read! Take up and read!" Whereupon he took up the scroll which lay at his friend's side, and his eyes came to rest upon the words: ". . . not in rioting and drunkenness, not in chambering and wantonness, not in strife and envying. But put ye on the Lord Jesus Christ, and make not provision for the flesh, to fulfill the lusts thereof" (Rom. 13:13-14). He read no further, but instantly, at the end of this sentence, a clear light flooded his heart and all the darkness of doubt vanished away. The church will never be able to evaluate this man's contribution as a result of this experience.[5]

Martin Luther was an Augustinian monk belonging to the sixteenth century. In November of 1515, he was serving as the professor of Sacred Theology in the University of Wittenberg, and delivering a series of lectures on the Epistle to the Romans. One phrase in the epistle kept intruding itself upon his consciousness: "the righteousness of God." Night and day he pondered its significance until at last he grasped the truth that it referred to that righteousness whereby, through grace and sheer mercy, God justifies men by faith. "Thereupon I felt myself to be reborn and to have gone through open doors into paradise." As a result, the whole of Scripture took on new meaning for him. And this led to his part in the Great Reformation.[6]

The Englishman John Wesley went rather unwillingly on a night in May of 1738 to a meeting in Aldersgate Street in London, where he heard the reading of Luther's *Preface to the Epistle to the Romans*. When he heard Luther's description of the change which God works in the heart through faith in Christ, Wesley recorded in his journal that he felt at that very moment a strange warming of his own heart. He felt that he had trusted in Christ, and Christ alone, for his salvation, and for the first time had assurance that his sins had been taken away, and thus was

5. Bruce, *The Epistle of Paul to the Romans*, p. 58.
6. Bruce, pp. 58-59.

saved from the law of sin and death. It was that event in the life of John Wesley that launched the great Evangelical Revival of the eighteenth century.[7]

Even Karl Barth, the great Swiss theologian of recent years, was moved by the message of the Epistle to the Romans. He declared that the mighty voice of Paul was new to him. What he heard and felt, he wrote down; and when it came to the attention of the theologians of central Europe, it fell like a bombshell on the theologians' playground. The effects of it are still being felt in the area where he moved.

These are just a few of the examples where notables have been amazingly changed by the message of the apostle Paul as recorded in the Book of Romans. If there were added to this the countless thousands of God's people whose names are unknown, but who have been just as profoundly moved into the experience of salvation, sanctification, and assurance, there would not be enough paper and ink to record their names and testimony. Who among God's children does not know Romans 1:16; 5:1; 6:23; 8:1, 28, 37-39; 10:9-10; 11:33-36; 12:1-2? Today, as never before, the influence of this book continues its triumphant course through the lives of men. May it never cease.

Questions for Individual Study

1. How do you think the apostle Paul was prepared to write the Epistle to the Romans?
2. When and how did the church begin in Rome?
3. Where did the apostle write this epistle and what was the approximate date?
4. What are some of the problems the scholars encounter as they study this epistle?
5. What experiences provided for Paul the occasion for the writing of this epistle?
6. Can you name some of the reasons that may have been in the mind of Paul for writing Romans?
7. Has this epistle had any wide influence on men? Has it affected your life in any way?

7. Bruce, pp. 59-60.

Chapter 1

Greetings and the Declaration of the Theme
Romans 1:1-17

I. GENERAL PREPARATION FOR THE STUDY

In addition to the brief introduction given in the opening chapter of this book, it seems wise to give some further information as the student approaches the immediate study of the text.

A. The position of Romans in the arrangement of the books in the New Testament is providential. In both Greek and Latin order it heads the list of the Pauline epistles. Even though it was not written first, it is regarded by all as the greatest of the Pauline epistles and gives a complete theological discussion of the Christian faith. The Latin order places this book immediately after the Book of Acts and thus it stands first among all the epistles.

The facts of Christianity appear in the Gospels and the Book of Acts. Next comes Romans, the inspired interpretation of these facts. At first this may not seem to be of importance. But after the passing of nineteen hundred years of church history, it is quite evident that its position is not by mere chance. A whole generation of liberal theologians has sought to bypass Paul and return to the facts to which they give their own interpretation. In this manner they are able to empty the facts of their value and intended blessing for men.

The cry of "back to the Gospels and the Acts" may at first sound pious and plausible, and most certainly it is important to keep the facts clearly in mind. But by a clever stratagem it is possible to insert mere human interpretation and by so doing empty those facts of their true meaning. For this reason God raised up a man by the name of Paul who received his interpretation of the facts by immediate revelation from God (Gal. 1:1, 16-17). The Book of Romans is the result, a theological treatise which puts all the facts in their proper relation to one another.

B. The gospel is the theme of this great book. That note is sounded in the opening words of the book (Rom. 1:1), and is followed to the very end of the book (16:25). To Paul this message is the "gospel of God" (1:1), "the gospel of his Son" (1:9), which he is ready to preach (1:15) and of which he is not ashamed (1:16). Because he is the channel of that message he calls it "my gospel" (2:16), and insists that the feet of those who preach it are beautiful (10:15). But unfortunately there are those who have not "obeyed the gospel" (10:16). Unbelieving Jews are enemies of the gospel (11:28). It rejoices his heart that God chose him, a Jew, to minister the gospel to the Gentiles (15:16); and he has bought up every opportunity in the eastern part of the Roman Empire to preach that gospel (11:19), and in places where no other man has gone (15:20). At this moment he is contemplating the journey to Rome where in the fulness of the Spirit he expects to preach the gospel to them (15:29). His parting thought in the epistle is a benediction "according to my gospel" (16:25).

The word *gospel* is not a theological term, nor is it a technical term, even though it has taken on such qualities. Frankly, it is a term that came right out of the common language of the people. The original Greek term was a word meaning "glad tidings" or "good news" (Luke 2:10). As a result of the conquests of Alexander the Great, the common language of the Greeks was spread from one end of what later came to be known as the Roman Empire to the other by 300 B.C. and continued to be the commercial language of the Roman Empire to about A.D. 300. This was a providential provision for the dissemination of the truth of the New Testament to the rank and file of the inhabitants of that day. As a result the word *gospel* became the medium to convey the message of God's grace to men.

Paul uses three expressions in the epistle in referring to the gospel. He makes it perfectly clear at the outset that as to source his message is the gospel of God (1:1). When he arrives at the point of describing its content he announces that its subject is Christ (1:16). Several times in the course of the epistle he clearly indicates that he is the servant of that message by speaking of "my gospel" (2:16; 16:25). He counted it high privilege to be the bearer of a message that had power to save both Jew and Gentile, because it revealed a righteousness that was available to all through faith. This righteousness by faith stood in marked contrast to that righteousness demanded by all other religions, a righteousness of men which at its lowest level men were unable to meet. It was this fact that made the gospel of Christ good news.

C. The writer took a text from the Book of Habakkuk, and with amazing skill unfolded its meaning in the Book of Romans. His text was Habakkuk 2:4, "The just shall live by . . . faith." Though it contains but three words in the Hebrew original and six in the English, the ideas are so arranged as to make this sentence provide a gospel with enough power to save the entire world. It speaks of righteousness in the phrase "the just." It speaks of life in the words "shall live." It marks the connection between the two. No righteous can die and no unrighteous can live. And to transform these possibilities into realities the condition is imposed in the words "by faith." When the lines of thought proposed in this text are projected into full argument, the Epistle to the Romans is the result. Study carefully the unfolding of the text in the exposition which follows.

D. The recipients of this letter are Christian people. They are the saints in Rome (1:7) immediately, and through them the other saints of that day and since. In a very real sense, then, this epistle is a church document. It is not a tract to hand to the unsaved, but a treatise to the saint. If the sinner asks, "What must I do to be saved?" he should not be told to read the Book of Romans. He should be told, even as Paul did the Philippian jailer, "Believe on the Lord Jesus Christ, and thou shalt be saved" (Acts 16:31). Salvation is not obtained by understanding a doctrine, nor having a correct theory of Christ's person, nor holding an orthodox view of the atonement. The only thing that is necessary is believing on the Lord Jesus Christ, and in so doing, yielding oneself to the measure of light he has concerning Christ. This does not mean that he does not need some light concerning Christ. But perhaps we shall all be surprised some-day to find out how little is necessary for exercising saving faith. But once such a man has actually experienced salvation, then he needs to understand the gospel by which he was saved. That is the purpose of the Epistle to the Romans: true doctrine concern-ing Christ and His salvation.

E. The general plan of this epistle is clearly recognizable. Expositors vary in the way they express this plan in words, but to a remarkable degree the words narrow down to the same mean-ing. The book begins with a formal introduction covering the first seventeen verses. Within these verses there are three movements of thought: first, an official introduction to the Roman church (vv. 1-7); second, a personal transition to the individual saints (vv. 8-15); and finally, the doctrinal affirma-tion of the Christian faith (vv. 16-17).

The argument of the epistle moves progressively forward to the conclusion beginning with chapter 1:18 and closing with chapter 15:33. Four great steps are discernible in the movement of thought: first, the adjudication of the wrath of God (1:18—3:20); second, the manifestation of the righteousness of God (3:21—8:39); third, the confirmation of the wisdom of God (9:1—11:36); and fourth, the transformation according to the will of God (12:1—15:33). The final chapter consists of saluta-tions, greetings, exhortations, and benedictions (16:1-27).

1. *The first movement of thought is the adjudication of the wrath of God* (1:18—3:20). This is a judicial decision handed down from heaven against the entire human race. The keynote is struck in the opening verse of the section: "the wrath of God is revealed from heaven" (1:18). This section is directed toward the question: Is the world of humanity really lost? The answer is conclusive and final. The entire world is guilty before God

(3:19). In the course of the unfolding of this section the apostle brings every class of mankind to the judgment bar of God and proves that each is lost. The pagan world of mankind is lost (1:18-32). The moral world of mankind is lost (2:1-16). The Jewish world of mankind is lost (2:17—3:8). The conclusion is inevitable—the whole world is lost (3:9-20).

2. *The second movement of thought is the manifestation of the righteousness of God* (3:21—8:39). Again, the apostle strikes the keynote in the opening verse of the section. "But now the righteousness of God . . . is manifested . . ." (3:21). That which until then existed, but was not known, is now brought out into the open and made clear and plain. Here is disclosed the method by which God saves men and women who are lost. He does this "through the redemption that is in Christ Jesus" (3:24). By justification God declares men righteous in Christ (3:21—5:21). On this basis God moves in sanctification and makes men holy in Christ (6:1—7:25). Throughout the entire experience God moves in preservation keeping believers securely in Christ (8:1-39).

3. *The third great movement of thought is the confirmation of the wisdom of God* (9:1—11:36). This is not a parenthesis. It is vitally associated with the theme of the gospel and appears at the proper point in unfolding the great logic of God's salvation for men. The keynote comes as a conclusion to the argument. It consists of an outburst of praise to God. "O the depth of the riches . . . of the wisdom . . . of God" (11:33). That wisdom was demonstrated in explanation of the reason why the nation of Israel has been temporarily set aside. The answer expresses how it was possible for Gentiles to come within the pale of God's blessing, namely, "that he might have mercy upon all" (11:32). There was a sovereign election of Israel (9:1-33). But there was a deliberate rejection of God's proffer on the part of Israel (10:1-21). Nevertheless, in merciful purpose, God promises a final restoration (11:1-36).

4. *The fourth and final movement of thought brings the argument to a climax, namely, transformation according to the*

will of God (12:1—15:33). The keynote is announced at the very
beginning. God's purpose is that saved men may be transformed
to prove His perfect will (12:2). Men are constantly asking how
saved men should live. The answer is clear. They should experience a progressive transformation by the renewing of the mind
(12:2). This will at last bring them into conformity to the image
of God's Son (8:29). This will be demonstrated in the individual
life of the believer (12:1-21), in the political associations with
the state (13:1-14), in the fellowship with other believers
(14:1-23), and in personal ministry in the course of life
(15:1-33).

The concluding chapter turns from the rather formal presentation of theological truth to the intimate and personal relations of
the apostle to this congregation. He recommends a dear sister to
them, Phoebe, who probably carried this epistle to them (vv.
1-2). Former experience with many in this congregation leads
him to send warm greetings to each one by name (vv. 3-16,
21-24). He cannot refrain from a warning of pious frauds who
would deliberately lead the saints astray (vv. 17-20). His heart is
full to overflowing, so he must end in a beautiful doxology to
God, the author of the gospel inaugurated in Christ, a secret
which is now revealed and experienced by the saints (vv. 25-27).

II. OFFICIAL INTRODUCTION TO THE CHURCH (vv. 1-7)

Paul did not establish the church in Rome, nor had he ever
visited it. Yet having been called of God and charged with
responsibility as apostle to the Gentiles, he did have authority in
relation to the church in Rome. Without hesitation and apology,
he announces his official position and relation to the church in
Rome. The opening sentence of the epistle is seven verses long
and consists of 126 words. By means of it Paul spans the gulf
between himself and this church, between the Jew of Tarsus and
the Christians of Rome. "Across the waters of national separation Paul has flung an arch whose firmly knit segments are
living truths, and whose keystone is the Incarnate Son of God.

Over this arch he hastens with words of greeting from his Father and their Father, from his Lord and their Lord."[1] This bridge consists of four great living truths: the servant of God, the gospel of God, the Son of God, and the saints of God.

A. The Servant of God (v.1). Note four great facts which the apostle affirms of himself.

1. *The writer introduces himself by the name Paul*, of Latin derivation meaning "small" (Acts 13:7). This name was probably given to him by his parents at birth, but did not become prominent until he began his ministry among the Gentiles (Acts 13:9).

2. *His position is that of a servant or slave in relation to Christ.* He regarded himself as bought with a price of precious blood and in deference to the One who purchased him he willingly became the Lord's slave (I Cor. 7:22-23). But being a slave of Christ meant the highest exaltation.

3. *His authority was that of an apostle.* The Lord had set him aside for communion with Him, and then had sent him forth with a commission (Mark 3:14).

4. *His appointment was by a sovereign act of the Lord Himself.* He was "separated," that is, quite literally "horizoned," marked out by clear lines of demarcation drawn by the Lord (Gal. 1:15; Acts 13:3). He did not acquire this position by ecclesiastical succession, congregational election, or self-appointment. He was therefore in no sense presumptuous in approaching this congregation of saints. He was operating within the authority that had been conferred on him.

B. The gospel of God (vv. 2-3). The moment Paul touches the phrase "the gospel of God" a whole succession of ideas flashes through his mind, and he must elaborate.

---

1. J. Agar Best, *St. Paul's Epistle to the Romans* (Hodder and Stoughton: London, 1902), p. 38.

1. *He insists that this is something that was promised by the prophets beforehand.* It is not something new, novel, or heretical.

2. *It is something that is recorded in the Scriptures of the Old Testament and can be researched, examined, and verified.* At least sixty-one passages from the Old Testament are cited in evidence in the course of this epistle.

3. *The Person of this gospel message is none other than the Lord Jesus Christ.*

C. The Son of God (vv. 3-5). It is this one Person who will fill the pages of this epistle. Essentially the gospel is Christ.

1. *His names are in striking order.* "Son" indicates His unique relation with the Father; "Jesus," His identification with mankind; "Christ," His messianic office and mission; "Lord," His absolute deity and sovereignty.

2. *He was made of the seed of David according to the flesh,* meaning that for the Eternal Son there was a change in the condition of His existence. Whereas He once existed only as God, now He not only continues to exist as God, but by a miracle of God has incorporated true humanity into the condition of His existence.

3. *He was declared the Son of God with power.* This means that He was marked out by sure signs of identity in His resurrection as possessing power inherent in the spirit of holiness that not only brought about His own resurrection, but also guarantees the resurrection of all those who are joined to Him.

4. *From Him Paul received three things:* the provision of salvation in grace, the position of apostleship, and the purpose to carry the gospel to the Gentiles.

D. The saints of God (vv. 6-7).

1. *Among all the called of Jesus Christ, Roman Christians are included, and to them Paul is now writing.* This means that God has already begun a work in them.

2. *They are beloved of God, not because of any personal merit, but nevertheless made the objects of the unsearchable riches of God.* These benefits Paul will unfold in the course of this epistle.

3. *By some amazing act of God they are called "saints."* They are far from saintly, but God has determined to call them saints. This will encourage them to bring their state up to their standing.

4. *Upon them Paul invokes the blessings of grace and peace.*

III. THE PERSONAL TRANSITION TO THE SAINTS (vv. 8-15)

The formal introduction is now completed (vv. 1-7). But there is more to be done in order to reach this group of Christian brethren in Rome. Authority must be implemented in order for it to be accepted. Paul feels that he must move beyond mere formalities to reach the hearts of these people. To accomplish this the apostle unveils the innermost recesses of his own heart and expresses his yearning for them. In seven steps he draws ever closer to them so that at last he can declare to them the basic purpose in writing this epistle.

A. He begins with thanksgiving for them (v.8). This conveys to them the fact that he recognizes the fact that they are gifts of God's grace. One quality about them elicited special mention: their faith. This probably has two aspects: the body of truth they held, and their own personal committal to it. Among believers throughout the whole world it was known and appreciated.

B. This opens the way for him to make reference to his own service (v. 9). The word for service points to religious service (cf. Heb. 9:1). God is witness to the fact that in true sincerity of spirit he is dedicated to the ministry of the gospel, whose object he has just spoken of when referring to their faith (v. 8).

C. This ministry brings him to his knees in prayer for them (vv. 9-10). As a very real part of this religious ministry he is to remember the brethren before the throne of grace. By name he is regularly imploring God on their behalf. Though he does this for them in his absence and supplements this ministry with this letter, he cannot rest until by the grace of God and according to His will he can actually visit them.

D. All this grows out of that earnest longing to see them (vv. 11-12). He is really homesick to see them, not for old time's sake, but because he wants to impart to them some spiritual gift. But he also recognizes that Christian fellowship is no one-way street. Where there is impartation there is also reception. It is always mutual. He will be able to confirm them in the Christian faith, and they in turn will comfort him.

E. To emphasize the sincerity of his longing to see them, he points to the frequency of his purpose to make the journey to Rome (v. 13). This purpose was genuine, for he made an effort to realize this ambition, but the Lord intervened and hindered by directing his journey elsewhere. Without a doubt the ambition of Paul to get the gospel to as many people as possible led him in his Christian calling to plan for Rome. At Ephesus some years before, this desire is recorded of him (Acts 19:21). During those dark hours in Jerusalem the Lord assured him he would get to Rome (Acts 23:11). But in spite of every effort on his part he met one hindrance after another (Rom. 15:22).

F. It was the heavy burden of indebtedness that constantly weighed on him to seek fruit among the Gentiles (vv. 13-14). Unworthy though he had been, someone was willing to bring the light of the gospel to him. Now he faces the same feeling of responsibility to get that message to others. Those who fall outside the pale of Israel, such as Greeks and barbarians, are eligible to hear the message. Intellectual attainment does not limit the need for the gospel; indeed, all need this message.

G. The fact that clinches this in the mind of Paul is readiness (v. 15). For whatever he is or has, he is now available for ministry to preach the gospel at Rome. The word "preach" in this case covers a wide area. It not only means conveying the gospel in its simplicity for those who have never heard, but also unfolding its depths to those who have already embraced its initial truths. Out of this will come fruit: fruit in the sense of maturing spiritual life as well as in the sense of multiplying the number of those who belong to the Christian community.

IV. DOCTRINAL AFFIRMATION OF THE FAITH (vv. 16-17)

The apostle has reached that point toward which he has been moving in this rather lengthy introduction. The transition is now completed and he can state the central point of the letter: *It is Christ who is the salvation of God*. The gospel of Christ is the good news about a person, the Lord Jesus Christ. With swift strokes of the pen, the apostle compresses into two verses the entire message of this book. Note these four things:

A. The personal declaration of appreciation (v. 16a). "For I am not ashamed of the gospel of Christ." This is the strongest possible recommendation for the message he bears. He is personally satisfied to the point that he is not ashamed to declare openly the value of this message. He was saved by it and he has lived by it for more than twenty years. It has carried him through every changing circumstance of life, and at no point has he been disappointed. Every claim has been verified and every promise of blessing has been fulfilled.

B. The central affirmation is clearly stated (v. 16b). "For it is the power of God unto salvation to every one that believeth; to the Jew first, and also to the Greek." This message is power, the kind that produces results. Its power resides in its meaning, and that meaning is centered in the person of Christ. It is accessible to all in that it may be appropriated by the exercise of personal faith. It issues in salvation, that is, deliverance which begins and never ends. It came first to the Jews and later expanded its borders to reach the Gentiles, so that now it is available to all humanity.

C. The essential explanation of its power (v. 17a). "For therein is the righteousness of God revealed from faith to faith." This is

Paul's way of saying that there is a righteousness of God that is available to men which meets all the requirements of God for full and complete salvation. The present tense of the verb "is revealed" indicates that there is a progressive unfolding of this experience in every life. From the moment of the initial act of faith, the believer moves out of one dimension of faith into another, continuously appropriating the righteousness of God to meet every need.

D. The Scriptural certification of this power (v. 17b). "As it is written, The just shall live by faith." The word "written" is in the perfect tense and means that it was written in the past and its validity remains in force. At that remote moment in Hebrew history when Babylon was moving down upon the little nation of Israel to crush it, it appeared to Habakkuk that all was lost. It was then that God encouraged him to write the words Paul uses as the text for this epistle (Hab. 2:4). Even though the darkness of sin has settled down upon the world and there is no hope for men, it is still true that "the just shall live by faith."

Questions for Individual Study

1. What importance should be attached to the position of Romans in the arrangement of the books of the New Testament?
2. What is the theme of the Epistle to the Romans? Can you cite passages that would indicate this?
3. What is the text of this epistle, and under what circumstances did it originate? Is it applicable in a situation such as confronted by this epistle?
4. Can you give the four major points in the plan of this book? Do they seem to be arranged in logical order?
5. Why was it necessary for the apostle to establish an official relation with the church in Rome?
6. In order to establish his authority to write to the saints in Rome, what other relationship was it necessary to cultivate so that Paul could be effective?

Chapter 2

The Judgment of God Upon the Entire World
Romans 1:18–2:16

At this point in the epistle the first main division of the argument begins. It deals with the adjudication of the wrath of God (1:18—3:20). This is divine judicial decision constituting a verdict against all mankind: "the wrath of God is revealed from heaven against all ungodliness and unrighteousness of men, who hold the truth in unrighteousness" (1:18). This means that all men are lost and in need of salvation.

This is the logical place to begin this theological treatise on the gospel of saving grace. Until it is clear that men are irrecoverably lost, there is no sound reason for discussing the way of salvation. In fact, no man is approachable with the doctrine of saving grace until he is convinced that he is lost, with no possibility of recovery within himself or his environment. Nor does Paul even intimate that this is a matter for debate. His utterances are declarative, positive, and final.

"Shall not the Judge of all the earth do right?" (Gen. 18:25). The answer to this is in the affirmative. God will do right, and He will therefore have a clear principle by which to evaluate the condition of man. In every case men will be found to fall short of that righteousness necessary to bring the approval of God, and that by their own choice. This defect renders them subject to the wrath of God.

Two principles are dealt with in the passage of Scripture set aside for this study. The first has to do with the revelation of God in nature, a revelation which is available to all men everywhere (1:19-21). The second is also true of all men to a greater or lesser degree. That is the revelation of God in conscience (2:1-16). Some loudly claim to be moralists with a sensitivity toward right and wrong (2:1). Others are not so willing to admit that they have a clear sense of right and wrong. At this point the judgment of God will take over (2:2-16). In either case God will judge men according to the light they have (Luke 12:46-48).

I. CONDEMNATION OF THE PAGAN WORLD (1:18-32)

The principle of judgment by which all mankind is now measured is the revelation of God in nature. Wherever men live, there is the earth beneath, the sky above, the sun, the moon, and the stars, and nature all about. No man is denied this revelation in its entirety, be he savage or civilized, rich or poor, educated or illiterate. The reaction of every man to God in view of this revelation renders him without excuse (1:21).

The apostle now brings indictment against mankind. He points out four things in the adjudication of wrath: It is revealed (v. 18), it is deserved (vv. 19-23), it is inflicted (vv. 24-31), and it is accepted (v. 32).

A. The wrath of God is revealed (v. 18). At least six things should be noted in this opening statement of the apostle Paul.

1. *The quality of this wrath is divine.* It is "the wrath of God." There is a whole list of adjectives that could be used to describe it. It will be holy, true, right, timed, infinite, incomprehensible.

2. *The source of this wrath is heaven.* This is a way of saying that there is supernatural control being exercised over everything, and in no sense is wrath to be interpreted as a fortuitous concourse of events (often called "calamity" on the human and natural level).

3. *The nature of this wrath is aversion to sin.* Two words appear in the Greek language that are rendered by the word "wrath." The one describes the sudden outburst of temper. The other points to slow and settled aversion. It is the second in this passage. God's wrath is the wrath of the court: slow, dispassionate aversion to sin and the determination to destroy it.

4. *The extent of this wrath is universal.* It is "against all ungodliness and unrighteousness of men." There is no detail that is swept under the rug or is conveniently ignored. Ungodliness is rebellion against the person of God. Unrighteousness is the transgression of His precepts.

5. *The time of this wrath is progressive.* The word translated "revealed" is a present tense and might be clearer if it were rendered "is being revealed." God does not settle all His accounts on Saturday night or at the end of the year. But there is payday someday, and this varies in relation to the issues at hand.

There is a revelation of God's wrath in nature. A curse fell upon it in the beginning because of the sin of man. Any defiance of the laws of God in nature takes its toll. There is a revelation of God's wrath in the Bible (Eph. 2:3; Rom. 6:23; John 3:36). Over and over again it warns man of judgment that may come now, and also that which will come ultimately (Luke 13:1-5). Moreover, there is a perfect revelation of the wrath of God in the cross of Calvary. There the full force of God's indignation against sin fell upon His infinite Son in a moment of time (Rom. 8:32; Matt. 27:36).

6. *The cause of this wrath is resistance to truth.* Here lies the very nature of sin. Men are determined to make themselves the supreme good and the chief end in life. And in order to achieve this end without a disturbing conscience they deliberately hold down or hold back the truth by means of their unrighteousness (II Tim. 4:3-4).

B. The wrath of God is deserved (vv. 19-23). The unfolding of this passage is marked by four movements of thought.

1. *All men had adequate opportunity to know God* (vv. 19-20). Even though God is invisible, God manifested Himself in the things He made. This means that He brought out into the open the things concerning Himself that until then existed but were not known, and He made them clear and plain. These necessary things He manifested to men: His eternity, His power, and His

Godhead. Men of very low intelligence are equipped with sufficient understanding to recognize that Someone made the things
of creation, that He had to possess power, and that He must be
eternal. This is sufficient to make all men without excuse in their
response to God.

2. *All men deliberately spurned this truth* (v. 21). The little
they knew about God was sufficient to lead them to glorify God—
that is, to recognize Him for what He is. And more than that, this
little that they knew was enough to make them realize that all
their benefits came from Him and called for thanksgiving. But
contrariwise, that is, in the face of this adequate knowledge, they
deliberately refused to recognize God; and they deliberately
refused to render thanks to Him for their benefits. In the place of
glorification and thanksgiving they became vain in their
thoughts. They turned to explanations that were absolutely useless, and darkness filled their hearts.

3. *All men engaged in insanity* (v. 22). "Professing themselves
to be wise they became fools." This means that they engaged in
self-serving exaltation. They called themselves wise. Out of the
word for "wise" comes the English word *sophisticated*. They
imagined that they knew more than they really did, and in
making this appraisal of themselves they engaged in a type of
insanity. The word for "fools" gives to us the word *moron*. Such
a one does not have the normal use of mental powers. In this case
men with normal mental powers, by an act of the will, turned
away from truth and thus descended to the same level as a
person without the use of average mental ability.

4. *All men progressed downward* (v. 23). The product of insanity is always something that contradicts reality. In this case it
was idolatry. Incapable of ignoring innate religious nature, they
exchanged the glory of God for that of man, then to birds and to
beasts, and finally to creeping things. Nothing in this account
suggests the evolution so widespread in the thinking of men
today. No archaeologist has been able to demonstrate that man
has made any progress upward in this area. But there is ample

evidence everywhere that there was a fall, and that since then men have ever descended to lower depths. The great descent here described is believed by some to have taken place after the Flood and is recorded in Genesis 11.[1] Paul saw it continuing in his day.

C. The wrath of God is inflicted (vv. 24-31). Where there is departure from the truth of God, there must inevitably be retrogression in life. This is the story of the gradual degeneration of the human race, and it runs true to form in every place on the face of the earth. The refusal to recognize God led to the refusal to respect the laws of nature. So God inflicted His wrath upon them by permitting them to go their way and reap the recompense for their deeds. Witness the unbridled descent to complete depravity.

1. *God gave them up to unimaginable impurity* (v. 24). The desires of their hearts led to all sorts of uncleanness in which they dishonored their own bodies among themselves.

2. *God gave them up to gross idolatry* (v. 25). They changed the truth of God into a lie, and as a logical sequel they worshiped and served the creature more than the Creator.

3. *God gave them up to unnatural sensuality* (vv. 26-27). Vile affections degraded womankind as well as mankind, so that they indulged themselves in lesbianism and homosexuality which brought immediate penalty on them, depicted in the destruction of Sodom and Gomorrah.

4. *God gave them up to complete depravity* (vv. 28-31). Inasmuch as they did not wish to retain any knowledge of God in their minds, God allowed them to fill their minds with things that were disapproved, the result of which is a list of sins that are utterly frightening.

1. Ben Adam, *The Origin of Heathendom* (Bethany Fellowship, Inc.: Minneapolis, 1963), p. 46.

D. The wrath of God was accepted (v. 32). Even though men knew that the course of sin they were following would end in judgment, they not only determined to pursue that path, but they even took pleasure in doing so and gave their consent to others who were following that path. As expressed by some, "We don't care what happens; we are determined to go our way."

There are some lessons to be derived from this passage of Scripture. It is clear that divine revelation is sufficient. Human sin is therefore deliberate. As an overview, it is evident that human development is downward and evil is progressive. Expulsion of the knowledge of God led to idolatry, idolatry led to sensuality, and sensuality gave birth to a whole brood of sins. "Sin starts from the neglect of light, followed by madness, idolatry, vice, manifold evil, and a malignant badness that takes positive satisfaction in wrong doing."[2]

II. CONDEMNATION OF THE MORAL WORLD (2:1-16)

The argument of the preceding Scripture passage places the entire pagan world under the sentence of judgment (1:18-32). The purpose of this passage is not to prove that men are sinners; that is taken for granted. The purpose is "to unfold the awful significance of it, in order to bring home to hearts and consciences the terrible results of sin in the certainty of God's judgment on unrighteousness."[3]

The movement of thought does not necessarily shift to another group of people in the passage about to be treated (2:1-16), but it does shift to another level or sphere of consideration. Whereas in the preceding passage the outward consequences of sin are set forth, in this passage the inward consciousness of sin is treated. Even men in the depths of sin, and as a result having darkened

2. W. H. Griffith Thomas, *The Devotional Commentary: Romans Vol. I* (The Religious Tract Society: London, n.d.), p 84.
3. Thomas, p. 87.

minds and hearts, still possess some awareness of sin. Enough light remains for them to evaluate the practices listed in the preceding passage and characterize them as wrong and condemn them. The exercise of this faculty constitutes one as a moralist (2:1).

When base sinners are able to recognize sin for what it is and characterize it as wrong and condemn it, it is a fair conclusion that the judgment of God will go farther than that (2:2-16). As John put it in his First Epistle, "If our heart condemn us, God is greater than our heart, and knoweth all things" (I John 3:20). Men in their pride may cleverly rationalize away their obligation to suffer the judgment upon sin, but the judgment of God no man can escape. It will follow the path of truth, measure precisely the deeds, ignore variations in persons, and penetrate to the secrets of men.

The order of this passage brings into view, first, the condemnation of the moralist by self-judgment (2:1); and second, the condemnation of the moralist by God's judgment (2:2-16).

A. Self-judgment of the moralist (2:1). Consider at least four things appearing in the opening verse of chapter 2.

1. *The man who is addressed.* "O man, whosoever thou art that judgest . . ." is the way it is stated in the text. This is not addressed to the Gentile exclusively, nor to the Jew. It is safe to say that it applies to any man within the scope of humanity who exercises the function of judgment. This could apply to the Jewish Pharisee, to the pagan philosopher, or to anyone whose enlightenment makes him capable of forming moral judgment. It is for all who can discern sin and judge it to be sin.

It is this sort of man who is properly called a moralist. Inasmuch as man was made in the image and likeness of God, even though that image has been marred by sin, there remains enough of the image so that men at the lowest level can recognize sin and condemn it. The Gentiles, who did not possess the written law of God, still were able to sit in judgment upon it and condemn it. Written indelibly on the conscience was a sense of that which is written in the law, and many strove after that righteousness (2:14-15).

2. *The method of confrontation.* At this point Paul employs a literary device often appearing in his writings. It is a type of composition which the ancients called *diatribe*, in which the author puts questions or objections into the mouth of an imagined critic in order to answer them. A pointed statement is made by one expositor:

> We know that there was another side to the pagan world of the first century than that which Paul has portrayed in the preceding paragraphs. What about a man like Paul's illustrious contemporary Seneca, the Stoic moralist, the tutor of Nero? Seneca might have listened to Paul's indictment and said, "Yes, that is perfectly true of great masses of mankind, and I concur in the judgment which you pass on them—but there are others, of course, like myself, who deplore these tendencies as much as you do."
>
> Paul imagines someone intervening in terms like these, and he addresses the supposed objector. . . . How apt this reply would have been to a man like Seneca. For Seneca could write so effectively on the good life that Christian writers of later days were prone to call him "our own Seneca." Not only did he exalt the great moral virtues; he exposed hypocrisy, he preached the equality of all men, he acknowledged the pervasive character of evil ("all vices exist in all men, though all vices do not stand out prominently in each man"), he practiced and inculcated daily self-examination, he ridiculed vulgar idolatry, he assumed the role of a moral guide. But too often he tolerated in himself vices not so different from those which he condemned in others—the most flagrant instance being his connivance at Nero's murder of his mother Agrippina.[4]

3. *The measure of judgment.* This is succinctly stated in the words of this verse: "for wherein thou judgest another, thou condemnest thyself." In the same measure that man pronounces judgment upon another, he is measuring his own failure at that point. The same degree of badness he attaches to it for another, he levels at himself. The same weight of judgment he insists should be inflicted on another, he is demanding for

4. F. F. Bruce, *The Epistle of Paul to the Romans*, pp. 86-87.

himself. Some men try to escape this issue by a pious with-drawal from judgment upon others, but the facts still remain that any judgment expressed or unexpressed places an individual in this position.

4. *The matter of judgment.* Note carefully where and why self-judgment is incriminating: "for thou that judgest doest the same things." Such a man is therefore inexcusable. The moralist is condemned by his own judgment—not because he exercises judgment, but because he does the same things. Failure to exer-cise judgment could be true for two reasons: either a man may be mentally bereft or morally insensitive. The first he cannot help; the second is blameworthy. For over and over again men are called on to make judgments, and in the very nature of man he is disposed to judge. In exercising judgment he needs to realize that he places himself under the sentence of God's wrath, for he demonstrates that he is lost.

B. God's judgment of the moralist (2:2-16). Men may uncon-sciously fail to grasp the significance of the point that Paul has just made. If so, there is a source of judgment which the moralist cannot escape—the judgment of God. Four aspects of God's judgment are presented by Paul.

1. *The judgment of God is according to truth* (vv. 2-5). This means that God's judgment always fits the facts. This will in-clude, as man looks at it, the minor sins as well as the major sins. This will cover the meanest and mightiest, the few as well as the many.

The moral philosopher, even though he seems to operate at a level above the average man, cannot hope to escape the judg-ment of God (v. 3). Any conclusion over that pattern is self-deception. Any man who engages himself in thinking of that type is indulging himself in the most extreme fancy.

On the one hand, a man like that is deliberately despising the riches of God's goodness and forbearance and longsuffering. It is the expression of these virtues in God that provides opportunity to such a man to come to repentance (v. 4).

On the other hand, a man like that is actually increasing the treasure of wrath he is laying up for execution in the future. It is hardness of heart and a rebellious spirit that leads him to imagine escape apart from finding refuge in the Lord Jesus Christ (v. 5).

2. *The judgment of God is according to deeds* (vv. 6-10). In this passage the apostle is not discussing the way to be saved or the way to be lost. That is taken for granted. The only way to be saved is by faith in Christ Jesus, and that is grace. The only way to be lost is to reject the grace in Christ Jesus. In this passage Paul is discussing judgment, which will be the evaluation of deeds for the corresponding degree of reward or punishment.

The saved man of verses 7 and 10 is one who persists in well doing. On the basis of his deeds at the judgment seat of Christ (II Cor. 5:10), he will be granted that degree of reward which corresponds with the degree of his deeds.

The lost man of verses 8-9 who is contentious, disobedient to the truth, engages in unrighteousness, and does evil, to this man at the Great White Throne (Rev. 20:11-15) there will be meted out that degree of indignation and wrath, tribulation and anguish which his deeds merit.

3. *The judgment of God is without respect of persons* (vv. 11-15). The statement of verse 11 is elaborated in the verses which follow and means that God is going to judge every man according to the light that was available to him.

In the good providence of God the Jews were given the law, a code which clearly outlined the terms of righteousness and the excesses of wickedness. Merely possessing the law will not be sufficient for them in the day of judgment. The issue will be whether they have kept it (v. 13).

The Gentiles did not receive the law in written form. But in some remarkable way God has written it on their hearts. The law of conscience will be the method of measuring their deeds when they come for judgment. Failing to live up to what they know will be the issue held against them (vv. 14-15).

4. *The judgment of God is according to Paul's gospel* (v. 16). At last God will examine men at the very center of their being. He will judge their motives. Human courts try desperately to get at these unseen motives that impel men to deeds, but only God is really able to get at the invisible cause of sin. The measure of the secrets of men will be the gospel which Paul preaches. Christ, the incarnate Son of God, is the center of that gospel. He went to the cross an innocent victim. But His going to that cross was necessitated because men had at heart the evil motive to exalt themselves to the place of supremacy, rejecting the supremacy of Christ.

> It is remarkable that precisely these four principles of judgment may be seen operating in every human court room worthy of the name, and in exactly the order in which Paul states them in Romans. The court will ask, first, "What is the law bearing on the case?" Second, "What did the accused do?" Third, "How much did he know about the law?" Fourth, "What was the motive in doing what he did?"[5]

Questions for Individual Study

1. What is the wrath of God as set forth in 1:18, and how is it revealed?
2. Why is this wrath of God deserved by mankind? What two sins constitute evidence?
3. In what ways is the wrath of God inflicted upon men? Upon the pagan world?
4. Can you explain what it is that constitutes a person as a moralist? Is he self-condemned?
5. What is meant when it is declared that God's judgment is according to truth and deeds?
6. In what sense is it true that God is no respecter of persons when He exercises judgment?

5. Alva J. McClain, *The Epistle to the Romans: Outlined and Summarized* (The Brethren Missionary Herald Company: Winona Lake, 1971), p. 18.

Chapter 3

5-29-77

Condemnation of the Jew and the Entire World

Romans 2:17–3:20

The movement of thought up to this point has demonstrated how completely men are lost. Even the believer in Christ needs to know this. It enables him to know from what he was saved and how utterly condemned he was, and how completely unable within himself or his environment he was to recover himself. It is this knowledge that enables him to appreciate the salvation of God in Christ. Though he may never have descended to the awful depths described in chapter 1, but for the grace of God he would have arrived at that place. This alone should be sufficient to arouse in him that insatiable restlessness for spreading the good news of salvation to others.

Reflecting back upon "the wrath of God revealed from heaven against all ungodliness and unrighteousness of men" (1:18), the believer cannot help but conclude that there was sufficient occasion for the gospel. With devastating logic the apostle has proved that the pagan world stands condemned for its failure to live up to the revelation of God in nature (1:18-32). And even where men have claimed some moral response in themselves to the demands of righteousness, they too stand condemned. By their own verdict they are condemned (2:1), and most assuredly they are condemned by the judgment of God because they have failed to live up to the revelation of God in conscience (2:2-16).

With the same logic the apostle invades the realm of the religious man and proves that he too is lost. By profession and practice the Jew stood separate from the Gentile nations; and because he had a God-given religion, Judaism, he lapsed into a condition of complacency concerning his own spiritual welfare. He not only had the revelation of God in nature and in conscience, but also the written revelation of God in the Old Testament. But this threefold privilege only left him thrice condemned (2:17—3:8). When this final protection is swept away, the apostle moves to the inevitable conclusion ". . . that every mouth may be stopped, and all the world may become guilty before God" (3:9-20).

I. CONDEMNATION OF JEWISH PEOPLE (2:17—3:8)

Though the apostle may have had the Jew in mind at some points in the preceding argument of the epistle, there is no doubt who is in his mind now. He addresses the Jew specifically. "But if thou bearest the name of a Jew . . ." (v. 17) is the way this passage begins in the American Standard Version. The key to this section is clearly the word "Jew" (2:17, 28-29; 3:1). All that appears in this section could apply only to the Jew. Because Jews are God-chosen people, does this mean they are better than Gentiles, and are safe from the wrath of God? Paul proceeds to travel swiftly and surely to the conclusion, "No, in no wise: for we have before proved both Jews and Gentiles, that they are all under sin" (3:9). With inescapable reasoning the apostle demolishes every protection behind which the Jew has sought refuge. Law, circumcision, birth, and argument leave the Jew utterly exposed to the wrath of God.

A. There is no refuge in the law (2:17-24). Zealous Jews listened to their learned rabbis as set forth in the Talmud, a record of their conclusions. In this commentary on the Old Testament, it is declared that a study of the law is equivalent to the keeping of all the commandments. Upon this the Jew rested (v. 17), meaning that upon the law he rested, leaned, refreshed himself—a sort of blind, mechanical reliance on the Mosaic law. He boasted of God as a national asset, of knowing God's will, of approving the things more excellent, because he was instructed out of the law. He made claims of himself in relation to others, such as being a guide to the blind, a light to those in darkness, an instructor of the foolish, a teacher of babes, because he possessed "the form of knowledge and of truth" in the law (vv. 18-20).

But of what value were all these claims? Was there any evidence that these claims had first of all been realized in themselves? By a series of questions addressed to the Jew, the answer to which in every case is negative, the apostle drives home the bitter conclusion (vv. 21-23). The Jew did not teach himself. He stole like Gentiles. He committed adultery. He engaged in idolatry. By breaking the law he dishonored God. Instead of being what he claimed in relation to the Gentiles, his conduct actually turned out just the opposite. "For the name of God is blasphemed among the Gentiles because of you" (v. 24 ASV). Jewish conduct led Gentiles to affirm untruth about God and the things of God.

B. There is no refuge in circumcision (2:25-27). The learned conclusions of the rabbis, as recorded in the Talmud, also said that Abraham sits at the door of hell and does not allow any to enter who are circumcised. In this rite the Jews trusted, just as many members of the church trust in the rite of baptism. But the fact is that rites do not safeguard anyone. Circumcision was an outward seal or evidence that a Jew belonged to the line of Abraham. But it was purely external. The real evidence of belonging to the family of Abraham was not circumcision, but the keeping of the moral obligations laid down in the law. Failure at this point only indicts the Jew and serves as evidence that inwardly he does not possess the nature of Abraham, nor is he subject to the authority of God in the law. For whatever reason the Jew submitted to circumcision, it was not because he bowed the knee to the law. Therefore his circumcision was a mere empty formality that had no meaning at all. It was really equivalent to uncircumcision.

The clarity of Paul's logic at this point unmasks the heart of the Jew and arouses his indignation. A Gentile, who makes no claims such as the Jew, when he keeps the righteousness of the law, even in uncircumcision, demonstrates a closer affinity to the law than does the Jew. His uncircumcision ought to be counted for circumcision. Certainly his nature is revealed by his keeping of the law and serves as condemnation of those who claim relation to the law and yet transgress it. The conclusion is this, that the circumcision of the Jew in which he trusted is without value, and the Jew is utterly defenseless. He therefore falls under the condemnation of the wrath of God.

C. There is no refuge in national birth (2:28-29). It was characteristic for the Jew to take refuge in his nationality. He loved to trace his lineage back to Abraham. In controversy with Christ, the Jews sought refuge in birth. On one occasion Jesus said to them, "And ye shall know the truth, and the truth shall make you free" (John 8:32). Immediately the answer came back, "We be Abraham's seed, and were never in bondage to any man: how sayest thou, Ye shall be made free?" (John 8:33). Then Jesus zeroed in on the real issue: "Verily, verily, I say unto you, Whosoever committeth sin is the servant of sin" (John 8:34). By this Jesus meant that they were not free. They were the bondslaves of sin. But this did not daunt them, so they made further claim to birth: "Abraham is our father" (John 8:39); to which Jesus replied, "If ye were Abraham's children, ye would do the works of Abraham. But now ye seek to kill me, a man that hath told you the truth, which I have heard of God: this did not Abraham" (John 8:39-40).

This provides the background for Paul's demolition of their false refuge in birth. Before God, birth must not only include outward physical features, it must also include inward spiritual nature. Even though a Jew may be able to trace his physical lineage back to Abraham, that is only part—and the least part—of this relationship. There must also be a spiritual relationship to Abraham. Circumcision in the flesh must be supplemented by circumcision of the heart, in the spirit, which the outward symbol is intended to portray. The fulfillment of the law in mere letter will never suffice with God, even though it may satisfy men. With God there must be a fulfillment of the law which reaches to the human spirit, and this will have praise of God. A true Jew is then one who belongs to the family of Abraham and also to the family of God (Rom. 9:6-7).

D. There is no refuge in argument (3:1-8). After the stinging indictments leveled at the Jew, as recorded in chapter 2, the apostle reproduces what most likely would be the argumentative response of the Jew. The key is in verse 5: "I speak as a man." He was once an unsaved Jew and he knows how he responded to the Christian faith. And without a doubt, more than once during the twenty years of his ministry he met the same response. The argument unfolds in four movements of thought.

1. *What is the use of being a Jew?* (v. 1). Is there really any advantage of being a Jew as over against being a Gentile? What profit accrues to the Jew when he submits to circumcision? If both Jew and Gentile end up under the wrath of God, then all the things the Jew counted worthwhile suddenly lose their value, and he has no position or standing that differentiates him from the Gentile.

The answer to that question, however, is clear (v. 2). The very fact that the oracles of God (the Bible) were committed to the Jew places him in an enviable position. God chose to reveal His mind to the Jews while the Gentiles remained in darkness. That is worth everything.

2. *What if some did not believe?* (v. 3). Though the central objection is in verse 1, and the answer in verse 2, the Jew now squirms in his discomfort and falls back on what Paul has already affirmed of the Jews, that they did not believe. If some did not believe, does that make the faith of God without effect? That is, since the Jew failed at his end, does that mean that God will turn back from His commitments?

To this objection the answer is a resounding No! (v. 4): "God forbid. . . ." God is true, though every man may be a liar. The confession of David in his great sin is used to substantiate the reply and refute this objection. This confession declares God righteous in all His promises and prophecies. In areas where men accuse God, He is vindicated (Ps. 51:4). The gifts and

calling of God are without repentance (Rom. 11:29). Though
men may be unfaithful, God is always faithful (II Tim. 2:13).

3. *Will not God be unjust to punish sin when it brings Him
glory?* (v. 5). This turn in the argument should unveil the amazing ingenuity of the human heart to justify itself (Jer. 17:9). It is
true that glory comes to God when He steps in and provides
salvation for the sinner. But it is not true that God excuses sin on
the one hand, nor that He dares to let sin go unpunished on the
other.

With all the force at his command the apostle repudiates such
a charge. "God forbid . . ." (v. 6). If such an argument as that
were to stand, it would mean that God could not judge the world.
And the Jew is only too convinced from his own Scriptures that
God will judge the world (Gen. 18:25; Deut. 1:17; Prov. 29:26).
Did He not judge the world at the Flood? Did He not judge the
cities of Sodom and Gomorrah? Moreover, Paul announced to
the philosophers on Mars' Hill that God would judge the world
in righteousness (Acts 17:31).

4. *If sin magnifies God's grace, why not commit sin?* (v. 7).
This quibble exhausts the treasury of Jewish argument. Of
course, the bestowal of grace in salvation upon the sinner brings
glory to God; but this does not provide a reason for indulgence in
sin. Still, like the Jew, there are those who would use this level of
argument to make provision for the flesh and to exonerate themselves from sin. As you can see, this is an attempt to put the
responsibility on God. It is an effort to establish a principle that
the end justifies the means. This would make God the author of
sin because He is the author of the principle, and thus man is
cleared of any guilt in wrongdoing.

The answer comes swift and sure (v. 8). It brands this sort of
thinking as pure slander—slander directed against the apostle
for preaching salvation by grace and slander against the God of
all grace. This final attack of the Jew upon the doctrine of
salvation by grace guarantees the truth of the doctrine of grace.
No other doctrine lends itself to this sort of slander. The doctrine

of salvation by works is not liable to such slander. But grace, because it does provide a refuge for the sinner apart from works and so completely removes all opportunity for boasting, arouses the proud heart. You can hear the sneer, "Let us do evil, that good may come."

For those who reason this way there is one last word. Their "condemnation is just." Two things ought to come home out of this truth. Strict legalism is sin and is based on spiritual blindness. This was true among Jews who sought to perform the works of the law and rejected God's grace. It is also true among those who make a profession of faith and imagine that mere performance of rites and ceremonies will commend them to God.

II. CONDEMNATION OF THE WHOLE WORLD (3:9-20)

Up to this point the apostle has been dealing with classes of people on the basis of the revelation God has given them. On the lowest level, the pagan, God has brought the witness of creation, the revelation of God in nature (1:18-32). On the next higher level, the moralist, God brings the witness of conscience, the revelation of God in the heart (2:1-16). On the highest level stands the Jew. Against him God brings the witness of Scripture, the revelation of God written (2:17—3:8). Now in this section God summons the entire world to the judgment bar, both Gentile and Jew.

> The procedure will be judicial, and the language like that of the courtroom. First, there is a general charge (9): all under sin. Second, there is a written indictment naming specific counts (10-18). Man is depraved in character (10-12), in speech (13-14), and in conduct (16-18). Third, there is a verdict (19-20): all the world . . . guilty before God. Against all this there is no defense; every mouth is stopped. Thus we have universal sin, universal guilt and universal silence.[1]

1. Alva J. McClain, The Epistle to the Romans Outlined and Summarized, p. 20.

A. The general charge against humanity (v. 9). Note the four things that make up this charge.

1. *The logic of the charge.* This centers in the word "then." It means "therefore." After having pursued the thought of the book to this point, in the course of which both Jew and Gentile have been placed under the wrath of God, the logical outcome is suggested, "Are we better than they?" or "Are we preferred?" The writer, Paul, identifies himself with Jewish people to whom he is writing, and ultimately with all Jewish people. Do all the special things true of Israelites make them to be preferred above Gentiles (Rom. 3:9)?

2. *The response to the charge.* "No, in no wise. . . ." No answer could be more absolute than this one. The original at this point consists of the word "no" and the word "all" fashioned into an adverb. Perhaps it could be translated, "No, completely," or "not at all." It sweeps away any possibility for the most minute excuse for being preferred above the Gentile. After the indictment of 2:17—3:8, it leaves the Jew in exactly the same place as the Gentile—subject to the wrath of God. Not any one of the special blessings bestowed on Jews clears him of guilt before God.

3. *The scope of the charge.* The language at this point is clearly that of the courtroom. The KJV reads, "for we have before proved both Jews and Gentiles, . . ." The ASV translates the same words, "for we before laid to the charge both of Jews and Greeks, . . ." The latter is to be preferred. "Laid to the charge" describes the act of placing a charge in the courtroom. Paul is insisting that he has already done that in the preceding argument. And this charge was leveled against both Jews and Gentiles, thus taking in all humanity.

4. *The seriousness of the charge.* The seriousness lies in the fact "that they are all under sin." He does not say that they are all sinners, nor that they have all sinned. He declares that they are *under* sin. This phrase gathers up all that goes with sin. This

includes its nature, its action, its power, its guilt, its condemnation, its doom. As a nature, it is not subject to God; in its fruitage, it gives birth to an unending brood of sins; as to power, it sweeps on with devastating force to destroy all in its path; as to its doom, even when confined at last in a lake of fire, there will be gnashing of teeth. All—not few, or some, or many, or most—but all are under sin.

B. The Scriptural analysis of the evidence (vv. 10-18). A cluster of Scripture passages is now presented to corroborate the evidence which supports the charge that all men are under sin (Ps. 14:1-3; 53:1-3; 5:9; 140:3; 10:7; Isa. 59:7-8; Ps. 36:1). Herein is a composite picture of all humanity. This does not mean that all these sins appear in each individual, but they do appear somewhere within the human family. And if men were allowed to go on, in the course of time each sin would appear in each individual. A fourfold picture of human depravity unfolds at this point:

1. *Humanity is depraved in character* (vv. 10-12). In support of the indictment that character is depraved, both negative and positive evidence is brought to bear.

On the negative side, "there is none righteous" (v. 10). This is the general state of mankind. Two details demonstrate this. "There is none that understandeth, and there is none that seeketh after God" (v. 11). Mental confusion about the relation of God to mankind and the universe is apparent on every hand. Moral exclusion of God from the thinking and practice of mankind follows immediately. Philosophically men may be said to seek after God, though never in such searchings have the philosophers found the God of the Bible. This, in itself, indicates that the one thread that could lead them to the true God has been completely ignored.

On the positive side, all men have declined from the divine pathway (v. 12). Two particulars are marshaled to substantiate this indictment. All have become utterly unprofitable and useless in the sense of fulfilling the divine purpose, namely, to glorify God and enjoy Him forever. And in addition there is not one that does good. From the standpoint of result, some men do good. And from the standpoint of means, it is true that some men do good. But from the standpoint of motive, there are none that do good. Whatever they have done is for some motive less than that of glorifying God. And even as to means and motive, no man has ever made a practice of doing good.

2. *Humanity is depraved in communication* (vv. 13-14). The description of man's condition reaches deeper than at first meets the eye. Corruption, deceitfulness, uncharitableness, and blasphemy are all exhibited in the speech of mankind. And these must all be traced to that inner source which is the heart. "For out of the abundance of the heart the mouth speaketh" (Matt. 12:34). A throat, like an open sepulcher, emits the stench and corruption of vile and filthy minds (v. 13a). Tongues that maneuver and manipulate the facts weave a fabric of deceitfulness and thus distort the truth (v. 13b). Beneath the lips lie the fangs filled with poison to inflict evil on friend or foe (v. 13c). The mouth is filled with everything designed to work havoc upon others: cursing, calling down evil on others, bitterness, dissatisfaction with everything in this life (v. 14).

3. *Humanity is depraved in conduct* (vv. 15-17). Three details are given to characterize the conduct of mankind in general. Everywhere you look these three things may be seen in greater or lesser degree.

As to the principle of existence, men are murderous; they do not hesitate to take life: "Their feet are swift to shed blood" (v. 15). The first son of Adam did not hesitate to take the life of his brother. This meant that he neither valued the source of life, the span of life, nor the benefits of life.

As to the arrangement of existence, men indulge themselves in "destruction and misery" (v. 16). One of the activities of life is productivity. This takes material resources and rearranges them for the benefit and happiness of mankind. But sinful human nature has left a trail of destruction and misery in its path. The achievement of centuries has suffered demolition in moments of time. And the destruction has left millions in sorrow and despair.

As to the harmony of existence, it is universally true of men that "the way of peace have they not known" (v. 17). From the beginning it was God's purpose that men should possess life, engage in productivity, and enjoy the fruits of their achievements in the atmosphere of tranquility. But not only have men not known peace with God, they have not enjoyed peace among themselves; and this fact has left them without peace in their own hearts.

4. *Humanity is depraved in cause* (v. 18). The apostle has left the source and explanation for all that precedes in this description of evil till the last:[2] "There is no fear of God before their eyes." This fear is that recognition, respect, and reverence for God that is essential for mankind to become subject to God. This lack of fear was first experienced in the Garden of Eden. Adam did not recognize God for what He is. He did not respect Him, and he did not pay Him reverence. Therefore he did not hesitate to reject God's command and walk in his own way. All of Adam's family has followed in his footsteps.

C. The deafening silence to the evidence (v. 19b). The trial is over, except for the defense. But to the amazement of all, there is no defense. There is uninterrupted silence. Every mouth is stopped. The world is guilty before God. And this guilt means not only that the world stands convicted, but is also obligated to suffer the penalty commensurate with the crime.

D. The irrevocable verdict of guilt (vv. 19-20). The law of God as written in the hearts of men and in the records of the Old Testament passes the final judgment. This law is the voice of God speaking. All it ever did was to give knowledge of sin, and in this case it has taken the measure of every man and now

---

2. W. H. Griffith Thomas, *The Devotional Commentary: Romans Vol. I,* p. 126.

pronounces him guilty. He is obligated to suffer the penalty which is death. No flesh is declared righteous by law-keeping. Law-keeping always fails, so that the law must finally pronounce the verdict of guilty and inflict the penalty of death.

Questions for Individual Study

1. In what sense did the Jew take refuge in the law, and how does this refuge disappear in the face of the facts?
2. What is the purpose of circumcision, and why does it fail to protect the Jew?
3. Why does the Jew seek refuge in national birth? Does it provide a refuge from wrath?
4. Can you trace the logic of the Jew as he resorts to argument to escape guilt?
5. What is the general charge laid against the world?
6. Describe the evidence Paul assembles to demonstrate the validity of the charge.

Chapter 4

6-5-77

Justification and Its Far-Reaching Results
Romans 3:21–5:21

Having finished his argument on the adjudication of the wrath of God (1:18—3:20), leaving the entire world under sin and with mouths stopped (3:19-20), the apostle has reached the point where he began (Rom. 1:17), and is now ready to unfold God's method in saving men. The first section of this epistle was absolutely essential to the argument. Until it was conclusively demonstrated that man is devoid of any righteousness that is acceptable to God, it was not clear that a divine righteousness was absolutely essential for salvation. Every sort of righteousness of which man is capable has been explored and has been demonstrated to fall short of the divine standard. This leaves man in utter despair, except for the fact that in the midst of this darkness there is a manifestation of the righteousness of God.

"But now apart from the law a righteousness of God hath been manifested . . ." (3:21 ASV). This is the key to this entire section (3:21—8:39). It answers the question concerning God's method in saving men, a method which is by "redemption that is in Christ Jesus" (3:24). Even though this righteousness existed before and had been appropriated by Old Testament saints, it was not manifested in fulness until Christ went to the cross. There it was brought out into the open and made clear and plain. All the types and shadows dealing with sin pointed forward to this event, but not until Christ actually died did this righteousness by faith take on life-size dimensions. "Abraham believed God, and it was counted unto him for righteousness" (Rom. 4:3). And "David also describeth the blessedness of the man, unto whom God imputeth righteousness" (4:6). But nothing would suffice to unveil this righteousness like the event of the cross.

There are three great movements of God in saving men, all three of these constituting the manifestation of righteousness (3:21—8:39). The first deals with justification, the act by which God declares men righteous in Christ (3:21—5:21). The second deals with sanctification, that work of God by which men are made holy in Christ (6:1—7:25). And finally, the third deals with preservation, in which men are kept securely in Christ (8:1-39). The first of these will constitute the area of discussion in this chapter, a discussion which is absolutely fundamental and foundational for all that follows.

I. THE DIVINE METHOD OF JUSTIFICATION (3:21-31)

The key to this section is the word "righteousness" (vv. 21, 22, 25, 26). Closely associated with this word are others from the same root in the original language, such as "justified" (vv. 24, 28), "justifier" (v. 26), "justify" (v. 30), and "just" (v. 26). As this discussion unfolds we shall note at least five things:

A. **Righteousness is manifested** (vv. 21-22). This manifestation took place at Calvary where it was made available to all men who would appropriate it by faith. This righteousness is apart from the law. The whole Old Testament witnessed to this righteousness by proclamation, promise, prophecy, picture, and portrayal, so that it is well established. What it needed was manifestation by divine act to confirm it in the minds of men. This is a righteousness of God which is available to men by the act of faith. This righteousness was provided by the work of Christ in satisfying the just demands of the law. He paid the full penalty of the law, and in doing so this deposit of righteousness is laid up and available to all who will exercise faith in the work of Calvary. By the act of faith this righteousness may be transferred to any person, Jew or Gentile, so that it becomes his own perfect righteousness.

B. **This righteousness is needed** (v. 23). "For all have sinned, and come short of the glory of God." This is true for the Jew. It is also true for the Gentile. It is true for all: "for there is no difference" (v. 22), "for all have sinned." The aorist tense, a constative in sense, makes the verb "sinned" a sweeping coverage of the entire human race in all its history.[1] All have sinned, whether once or a thousand times, and therefore have disqualified themselves for any blessing from God. But there is more evidence for need of this righteousness. "Come short" is a present tense indicating the fact that they are continuously falling short of the glory which is acceptable to God. There are greater and lesser sinners. But when they attempt to span the broad ocean expanse between man and God by a leap of human righteousness, all are falling short, scarcely leaving the shore on the near side. And this is continually going on.

C. This righteousness is provided (v. 24). Because so much is wrapped up in this one verse it deserves careful explanation.

1. The meaning of justification. This is centered in the word "justified." Because there are those theologians who have interpreted this to mean "to make righteous," it is necessary to point clearly to the use of the word. If the meaning "to make righteous" were used in the place of the word "justify" in such texts as Romans 2:13; 3:4; Deuteronomy 25:1; and Luke 7:29, it would become obvious that any such definition is ridiculous. However, to understand that the word means "to pronounce righteous and treat as such," that meaning is clear. Using this meaning in such passages as Job 13:18 and 25:4 makes sense. Such is its meaning in Romans.

But the matter is not that simple. For a human judge to pronounce a man righteous who is righteous is an easy matter. But consider the kind of people God must pronounce righteous. He deals only with sinners and the ungodly. Since God considers it an abomination for a human judge to justify the wicked (Prov. 17:15), it is not surprising to hear Him declare that He will not justify the wicked (Exod. 23:7). But God does justify the wicked,

---

1. A. T. Robertson, *Word Pictures in the New Testament, Vol. IV* (Richard R. Smith, Inc.: New York, 1931), p. 347.

as clearly set forth in the Book of Romans. This calls for an explanation.

2. *The manner of justification.* Simply stated, the manner is expressed in the word "freely." The word in the original comes from a root meaning "to give." Quoting from the Old Testament concerning Himself, Christ said, "They hated me without a cause" (John 15:25). That is, there was no cause in Christ why they should have hated Him. In this passage it means that there was nothing in sinners serving as a cause why God should declare them righteous. Not even the faith they exercised to appropriate the benefits in Christ constituted a cause. Faith possesses no intrinsic value. It is merely the hand that reaches out to accept the benefit.

3. *The source of justification.* The source is attributed to "grace." The word has such a large and wonderful usage it can hardly be overestimated in relation to salvation. It points to the undeserved, unmerited favor which God bestows on sinners. But it means more than that. It is a favor which God bestows on sinners in spite of their merit. They do merit something: judgment. It is even more than that. It is a favor God bestows on sinners without any thought of pay in return (Luke 6:31-35). Every time the word "thank" appears in this passage it is the translation of the word "grace." Read the word "grace" instead and it will give you a new conception of God's grace. On the human side there was no cause in us for justification, but on the divine side there was an unlimited supply of grace.

4. *The ground of justification.* This is "through the redemption that is in Christ Jesus." This means that there had to be a redemptive price paid to set the sinner free. While it did not cost us anything, it cost God everything. Christ stood in our stead and suffered our doom. He went out into the darkness and suffered separation from God. That explains the cry of desolation at the cross: "My God, my God, why hast thou forsaken me?" (Matt. 27:46). There is no explanation for that piercing cry except that He laid down His life in our stead. That was what it took to

satisfy a holy God in His indignation against sin. Otherwise Christ died without a cause (Gal. 2:21). "For he hath made him to be sin for us, who knew no sin; that we might be made the righteousness of God in him" (II Cor. 5:21).

D. The righteousness of God is demonstrated (vv. 25-26). Here a special effort is made by the writer to provide for clear thinking on the part of the reader. So it is necessary to point out now that the word "righteousness" is used in two different senses in this context. Up to this point the writer has been talking about a righteousness of God which is transferable by faith. But in verses 25-26 Paul introduces a righteousness of God that is non-transferable. It is the attribute of righteousness which belongs alone to God and cannot be given to another. It is this righteous attribute that had to be established when God made provision to justify sinners. Several points need further discussion.

1. *A demonstration of God's righteousness was made at the cross.* Twice in these two verses the word "declare" appears. It is a word which means to put on display or exhibition directed to a point. It means pretty much what our word *indicate* signifies. This display is public in nature for the purpose of capturing the attention and directing the thinking of people. In each verse (v. 25, v. 26), its end result is to exhibit "his righteousness." If there is any such thing as salvation it must come from God, and God must be consistent with Himself. He cannot be like the gods of the pagans, demanding righteousness on the one hand and denying righteousness on the other.

2. *Propitiation was the means of displaying the righteousness of God.* This sets forth the divine aspect of the atonement.[2] The word "propitiation" used in this verse refers to the place where propitiation is made. In the temple this was known as the mercy seat (Heb. 9:5). The mercy seat was behind the veil within the holy of holies where only the presence of God was manifest. The

2. W. H. Griffith Thomas, *The Devotional Commentary: Romans Vol. I*, p. 143 ff.

propitiation placated or appeased the wrath of God and it was unnecessary for anyone else to observe. But now God determined to make a public demonstration of the placating of His wrath, and Jesus Christ was to be the place where that was made. God alone was able to placate His righteous wrath against sin; so the entire operation of propitiation is supernatural and divine. Christ *made* the propitiation (Heb. 2:17 ASV), Christ *is* the propitiation (I John 2:2; 4:10), and Christ is *the place* where the propitiation was made (Rom. 3:25).

3. *The passing over of past sins was one reason for making propitiation.* In all the ages from Adam to Christ the sins of men had only been passed over. "Remission" translates a different word in this verse than elsewhere. Here it means "to pass over" or "suspend judgment" (Acts 17:30 ASV). In the longsuffering and forbearance of God a covering was provided in the sacrifices for sin. But in none of them was there any expiation of sin. To satisfy God's holy aversion to sin, "it is not possible that the blood of bulls and goats should take away sins" (Heb. 10:4). Therefore, until propitiation was made, there was always the lingering thought in the minds of men that God is not a God of righteous judgment (Mal. 2:17). But at Calvary, in the person of Christ, propitiation was made and put on display before the entire world.

4. *Justification by faith in the present provided another reason for making propitiation.* God's supreme desire from this point on was to declare men righteous by faith. But His act must also provide clear demonstration of the fact that He Himself does not violate His own righteousness. Propitiation made this possible. His righteousness is demonstrated by satisfying the just demands of that righteousness in propitiation. At the same time it opened the way for Him to declare righteous every man who would appropriate the benefits of propitiation in Christ by faith.

5. *The proper time for propitiation had arrived.* "At this time," or more literally, "in the now time." Now was the proper time for propitiation to be made. The word for "time" always

points to the fit, suitable, proper time for a thing to occur. And we may be sure that God is always on time. "But when the fulness of the time was come, God sent forth his Son, made of a woman, made under the law. To redeem them that were under the law . . ." (Gal. 4:4-5). It was at this time that God made public demonstration for the entire world that He had appeased His own wrath against sin. This provided the good news to Jew and Gentile alike that He would receive anyone who in simple faith would appropriate the benefits of this propitiation.

E. The righteousness of God is vindicated (vv. 27-31). Contrary to what men were saying in the day of Paul and since, there are certain advantages which grow out of this method of justifying men.

1. *It excludes boasting* (vv. 27-28). When men are saved completely by the work of God in grace, there is no provision made for human boasting. Faith only appropriates what God has provided and it makes no provision for human works. Where human pride is involved, this goes down hard. For one of the aspects of the sinful nature is its insurgency against God. It desires to be thought of more highly than it should, and this is sin. So faith excludes the sin of boasting.

2. *It includes all men* (vv. 29-30). The Jews would have liked to exclude Gentiles as proper recipients of God's salvation. This was contrary to the teaching of the Old Testament. But long years in separation from Gentiles had developed this false idea. However, with this new revelation concerning salvation, it was established that since God was Lord of both Jew and Gentile, there could be only one way of justifying each.

3. *It establishes the law* (v. 31). Though men had thought to establish the law by imposing the demands of the law, in no case was there ever a man who kept all the law, all the time, always perfectly. This could only mean that any salvation based on the works of the law was a violation of the law. But the one pro-

pitiation of Christ satisfied the full demands of the law once and for all. Appropriation of this by faith established the law.

II. THE HUMAN ILLUSTRATION OF JUSTIFICATION (4:1-25)

For the Jew in particular, but also for the Gentile, there may be real value in relating the principle of justification by faith to Abraham. He is the father of the Jews and also the father of the faithful (4:1, 16). So the apostle Paul devotes a whole section to a discussion of this principle in relation to Abraham. It develops that three distinct blessings came to Abraham by faith (4:1-2).

A. Abraham received righteousness by faith (vv. 3-12). Two movements in the argument settle the matter so far as Abraham is concerned.

1. *First, the absolute explanation is cited from Scriptures* (vv. 3-8). The historical account is recorded in Genesis 15:6 and repeated by Paul in verse 3. Abraham believed God and it was counted to him for righteousness. This meant that righteousness came to Abraham by grace (v. 4), and that it was faith which appropriated it (v. 5). The experience of the great king of Israel, David, is cited as further evidence in support of the proposition (vv. 6-8; cf. Ps. 32:1-2).

2. *Second, the apparent objection also closely associated with Abraham is dealt with* (vv. 9-12). Did this righteousness come to Abraham when he was in uncircumcision or in circumcision? If the rite of circumcision, a definite work of Abraham, possesses inherent efficacy, then the righteousness should have come after circumcision (vv. 9-10a). Scripture, however, makes it clear that it was while he was in uncircumcision (vv. 10b-11a). The purpose was that he might be father also to them who were uncircumcised (vv. 11b-12), and circumcision was merely an outward seal (v. 11a).

B. Abraham received 'an inheritance by faith (vv. 13-16). Again two main ideas are presented for the reader's consideration.

1. *Faith appropriated the promise* (vv. 13, 16). The world was promised to Abraham, the central part of which was to be the homeland of the Jews (Gen. 15:18). And this was appropriated through the righteousness of faith. So the provision is one of grace reaching all the seed of Abraham—Isaac immediately, Israel more remotely, Christ preeminently, and all believers ultimately (Ps. 72:8; Dan. 7:27; Zech. 14:9; Matt. 5:5; Rev. 5:10).[3]

2. *Law would have invalidated the promise* (vv. 14-15). If the heirs were those who lived by law, then faith is immediately excluded, and the promise is of no effect because the promise operated on the condition of faith. Any promise based on law would have ended up in wrath with no one to inherit the promise. But at the time this promise was given there was no law to measure transgression. Actually, the law did not come till 430 years later (Gal. 3:16-18).

C. Abraham received a posterity by faith (vv. 17-22). Note two movements of thought in the verses which follow.

1. *The promise of seed* (vv. 17-18). The promise is clearly rooted in the historical account of Abraham recorded in the Book of Genesis (Gen. 15:5; 17:4-8). His seed was to be numerous. They were to constitute many nations. They would inherit the earth. At the time this promise came, Abraham had no child (Gen. 15:2-4). The only tangible thing he had to hold onto was a God "who quickeneth the dead, and calleth those things which be not as though they were" (v. 17).

2. *The possibility of failure* (vv. 19-22). On the human and natural level the circumstances were all against the fulfillment of this promise. Abraham had reached that age when fertility of the male ceases. And his wife Sarah was in a similar condition; she was unable to bear children. But in the face of these circumstances Abraham did not waver back and forth between these two alternatives. He set his face toward the promises of God and

3. George N. H. Peters, *Theocratic Kingdom, Vol. II* (Funk and Wagnalls: New York, 1884), p. 577.

his faith took on power, giving the glory to God; and he was fully
assured that the One who made the promise was able to bring it
to completion. It was not until twenty-five years later that Abraham entered into the realization of the promise.

The final words of this chapter are in summary of the value of
the principle of faith (vv. 23-25). The Old Testament record
gives due credit to Abraham, but the record was also intended to
give encouragement to his seed who believe on Christ. He died
for our offenses, and He was raised to demonstrate that faith in
Him declared us righteous.

III. THE CONSEQUENT BLESSINGS OF JUSTIFICATION (5:1-11)

Justification is the initial and foundational blessing in salvation. But with it comes a whole host of blessings which the
writer now enumerates. He does not attempt to name all of them,
but he does point out those blessings that are essential and
important to the full enjoyment of the Christian faith. This entire
passage is declarative in sense, acquainting the believer with the
spiritual blessings which became his at the moment he placed
his faith in Christ.[4]

A. Peace with God (v. 1). The state of hostility which once
existed between God and man is now over for the believer. The
two are at peace.

B. Access by faith (v. 2). A rebel may be pardoned but have no
access into the presence of the king, but we have access into His
holy presence.

C. Standing in grace (v. 2). This is a perfect standing provided
by grace. It is as perfect as Christ, for we are accepted in the
beloved (Eph. 1:6).

4. Kenneth S. Wuest, *Romans in the Greek New Testament* (Wm. B.
Eerdmans Publishing Company, 1955), pp. 75-77.

D. Rejoice in hope (v. 2). Our joy lies in the hope that we shall shortly be conformed to the image of Christ, who is the glory of God (Rom. 8:29; John 1:14).

E. Rejoice in tribulation (v. 3). Where once tribulation was bitter and hurtful, by the power of God such is made to work for good (Rom. 8:28).

F. Tribulation worketh patience (v. 3). The effect of tribulation on the saint is to encourage him in greater persistence in the Christian faith.

G. Patience issues in experience (v. 4). As persistence pushes the believer forward in the Christian faith, it only serves to usher him into a new and more blessed experience of the Savior.

H. Experience issues in hope (v. 4). The more experience there is in the Christian life, the brighter shines the hope of its future consummation.

I. Hope maketh not ashamed (v. 5). Hope is that expectation of future reality not yet experienced. Its contemplation brightens the face and makes the heart glow with enthusiasm.

J. Love of God is in the heart (v. 5). Where once there was hatred and malice, now there is that love of God that sets itself upon its object to do it good; and we are that object.

K. The Holy Spirit is given to us (v. 5). Unsaved men live totally apart from God. But once saved, the Spirit of God takes up His dwelling in them.

L. Proof of God's love for us (vv. 6-8). Whereas there are few who will die for others, even for a good man, Christ did more. He died for ungodly sinners.

M. Immunity from wrath (v. 9). Justification established peace between God and us. Therefore in the end-time judgments of wrath, we shall also be saved from them (I Thess. 1:10; 5:9).[5]

5. F. F. Bruce, *The Epistle to the Romans*, p. 124.

N. Assurance of final salvation (v. 10). Reconciliation resulted when Christ died for us as enemies. But now as His own, His high priestly ministry will carry us through to the end.

O. Rejoice in God Himself (v. 11). As a result of justification, the believer rises to that pinnacle where he rejoices in the person of God Himself (Rom. 11:33-36).

You cannot miss the movement of the argument in this paragraph. Justification, which delivered us from condemnation in the past, and is delivering us from all fear and doubt in the present, guarantees the completion of salvation in the future.[6] Justification is therefore the first fundamental of the Christian faith.

IV. THE INAUGURATION OF A NEW RACE BY JUSTIFICATION (5:12-21)

A. The progression of thought to its conclusion. "Wherefore," the first word of this section, means "on account of this" or "because of this." It marks the connection with what precedes and the transition to what follows. The preceding section made it clear that justification takes the sons of Adam from that place where they departed from God and brings them back to God, so that now they "rejoice in God" (5:11 ASV). The argument of this section is therefore fundamental to all that will follow in this epistle.

B. The presentation of the two heads. Rooted in the problem of sin and righteousness is the relationship to the heads of two races. In this section Paul unfolds an idea which was first stated in his epistle to the Corinthians (I Cor. 15:45-47), the first Adam and the Last Adam. Each is the natural head of a race, and in this section the apostle points to the solidarity of the race. Whatever was in the first Adam is bound to appear and expand in the development of his race (v. 12). Since Adam is the figure of Him

---

6. Thomas, *The Devotional Commentary: Romans Vol. I,* p. 199.

to come, Christ, it follows that whatever is in Christ will eventually appear and expand in the development of His race (v. 14).

C. The procession from the first Adam. Throughout this section there is a sorrowful unfolding of the things that proceed from the first Adam to his race. There is sin (v. 12), disobedience (v. 19), transgression (v. 14), offense (v. 15), condemnation (v. 16), judgment (v. 18), and death (vv. 12, 14, 21). The entrance of the law did not change this growing harvest of woes proceeding out of the first man, Adam (vv. 14, 20). It only made sin more conspicuous and dreadful. The entire race united to Adam was inevitably headed toward that final night of separation from God in the lake of fire (v. 21).

D. The prospective from the Last Adam. With bold strokes of the pen the apostle marks out the triumphs of the present and of the future for those who are joined in the new race to the Last Adam, Christ. Just "as all the evils of the race have sprung from one man, so all the blessings of redemption have come from one Person and one act."[7] There is obedience (v. 19), grace (v. 15), a free gift (vv. 15, 16), justification (v. 18), righteousness (v. 18), life (v. 17), and eternal life (v. 21). Wherever sin flourished, grace exceeded it (v. 20). Though sin has exercised a rule to death, grace overcame it and reigned through righteousness to eternal life (v. 21). The final word explains how—by relation to Jesus Christ our Lord (v. 21).

Questions for Individual Study

1. What is the difference between a righteousness of God that can be transferred and a righteousness that cannot be transferred?
2. What does Scripture mean when it refers to justification by faith? What is justification?
3. What is the meaning of propitiation? Who does the propitiating, and who is propitiated?
4. What are some of the benefits that are direct results of justification by faith?

7. Thomas, p. 204.

5. What great historical instance is cited of justification by faith? What did he get as a result?

6. What are some of the blessings that come with justification by faith? To what end do these blessings bring the believer?

7. Why does Paul finally resolve the discussion on justification by bringing Adam and Christ into the picture?

Sanctification and Its Immediate Blessings
Romans 6:1–7:25

There is no break in the argument of the epistle as the apostle moves from the thought in chapter 5 to that in chapter 6. But there is transition to a new and succeeding area of truth relating to the salvation of the believer. The recognition of this fact is absolutely essential in understanding the provision God has made for the complete and satisfying experience of salvation. Justification, that act of God in declaring men righteous and treating them as such, as set forth in 3:21—5:21, is foundational to the truth that is now being introduced into the argument. It is not to be confused with it on the one hand, nor is it to be ignored as preparation for it on the other.

The exposure of man to the wrath of God as set forth in the opening division of this book (1:18—3:20) has been dealt with in the provision God has made in justification in the next section (3:21—5:21). On the basis of the redemption that is in Christ Jesus the guilt and penalty of sin was settled by a judicial act. On the condition of faith men were declared to be righteous and God treats them as such. This standing in righteousness is permanent. There is nothing that can be added to this, and nothing can be taken away. But there is another problem that immediately confronts the thinking man, and that is the problem of sin in the life of a justified man. Any thinking man cannot help but raise the question in his thinking—"But where do we go from here?"

The problem of the power and practice of sin in the life of the justified man is therefore the subject that is now introduced into the argument. This is obvious from the way the chapter begins. "What shall we say then?" (6:1). Say to what? The only possible answer must be that which has immediately preceded "Shall we continue in sin, that grace may abound?" (6:1). The question surely points back to the statement in 5:20, "But where sin abounded, grace did much more abound." An enemy of justification by pure grace on the one hand, or a confused believer on the other hand, could easily raise the question, "If the grace of God is greater than the sin of man, why not keep on sinning?" To this question chapters 6 and 7 are directed. These chapters deal with that phase of salvation called sanctification, dealing with the power and practice of sin. The positive aspects of sanctification are set forth in chapter 6; the perilous aspects of sanctification are set forth in chapter 7.

I. THE POSITIVE ASPECTS OF SANCTIFICATION (6:1-23)

It was declared of Christ at His birth, "thou shalt call his name Jesus: for he shall save his people from their sins" (Matt. 1:21). Note carefully the preposition "from" their sins. It is not in their sins. Two aspects of sin are therefore named in chapter 6 from which salvation is intended to save them. One is the continuation in sin (v. 1); the other is the single act of sin (v. 15). In verse 1 the tense of the verb "continue" is present, pointing to a habit or practice of sin. In verse 15 the tense of the verb is aorist, pointing to the single act of sin. In both, the issue is the same. Does the fact that we have entered the sphere of grace and are no longer under bondage to the law mean that we are free to live in a course of sin or even to engage in the act of sin?

The answer to both is a vigorous and absolute "no," "God forbid" (vv. 2, 15). The thunderous "no" constitutes the immediate answer to these questions; but the solution is to be found in the right way of sanctification, which is the way of holiness. With this theme the entire sixth chapter is occupied. As will be noted by following the movement of thought in the chapter, two problems are dealt with. The first problem is dealt with in verses 1-14; the second problem is dealt with in verses 15-23.

A. The justified man cannot continue in sin because of identification with Christ (vv. 1-14). We shall note three things.

1. *The problem of continuing in sin* (vv. 1-2). Consider carefully the significance of the question with which this chapter begins. It is vitally associated with verse 20 of the preceding chapter. If it is a principle with God that a superabundance of grace results out of living in sin, then why not continue to live in sin so that grace will abound in pardoning sin more abundantly? Why take one out of the realm of sin if that is the realm where grace abounds?

This question makes it perfectly clear that justification does not mean to make righteous.[1] For if that is what it means, this question would be superfluous, pointless. But the facts are, justification means "to declare righteous"—to declare righteous the kind of men who are unrighteous and remain so, even though God calls them righteous and treats them as such (4:5). As it stands, the question is important and insists on an answer.

The immediate response is with a burst of scorn. "God forbid. . . ." Let it not be so. "How shall we, that are dead to sin, live any longer therein?" Thus Paul denounces the question as impious before moving against it in refutation. Only an evil heart would respond this way toward the grace of God. This is turning the grace of God into lasciviousness and deserves the indignation of the apostle. True morality is not only not placed in jeopardy, but is actually promoted by the grace of God.[2]

2. *The principle of identification with Christ* (vv. 3-13). The way of holiness may be outlined and summed up in four words found within these verses: "know," "reckon," "yield," and "obey."[3]

---

1. W. H. Griffith Thomas, *The Devotional Commentary: Romans Vol. II*, p. 6.
2. H. P. Liddon, *St. Paul's Epistle to the Romans* (Longmans, Green, and Company: London, 1893), p. 108.
3. Alva J. McClain, *The Epistle to the Romans Outlined and Summarized*, p. 27.

First, *the believer needs to know certain facts about identification with Christ* (vv. 3-10). Notice the presence of the word
"know" in verses 3, 6, and 9. By union with Christ believers
died, were buried, and rose when Christ died, was buried, and
rose again. The "baptism" of this passage speaks of that spiritual
union with Christ. This is not baptism in water, but baptism into
Jesus and into His death, of which water baptism is the symbol.
Though it is true that Christ died *for* sin, in this passage it is
talking about dying *to* sin (vv. 2, 6, 10). This means that death
severed the connection with sin. Death renders the body or
principle of sin inoperative (v. 6). That is the meaning of the
word "destroyed." In such a situation it is no longer possible for
the dead man to do any service to sin. He is freed from sin (v. 7).
Christ rose from the dead, and from that point on death has no
more dominion over Him, for He died unto sin once. Now He
lives to God (vv. 9-10). Since the believer is identified with
Christ, the same thing is true for the believer (v. 4).

Second, *the believer should reckon these facts true concerning himself* (v. 11). Just as Christ in fact died and was separated
from sin and now lives to God, so also the believer should
consider it a fact; for indeed it is a fact that he died to sin and
lives to God. In view of the fact that the believer was united with
Christ in death, burial, and resurrection, it is his obligation to
reckon it as true; for it is true that he actually died, was buried,
and rose again in Christ.

It is important for the believer not to draw any false conclusions from the statements of the text. No mere subjective view
of death as having taken place in the heart of the believer is here
being taught. When it speaks of "dead to sin," this does not
mean the death of sin as a power in the heart. The writer does not
say sin is dead to or in us. He says that we are dead to sin, and we
are to keep on considering this to be true by faith, for it is true in
fact.

Third, *believers must yield themselves and their members to
God* (vv. 12-13). The word "yield" is elsewhere translated by the
word "present" (Rom. 12:1), and in this form lends more of the

active and positive sense intended by the author. On the negative side, sin should not be allowed to reign as king in the mortal body of the believer to the end that the believer obeys it in the satisfaction of the lusts (v. 12). The believer should not present his members as weapons of unrighteousness to serve sin (v. 13a). On the positive side, believers should present themselves to God as alive from the dead and their members as weapons of righteousness to God (v. 13b).

Fourth, *the believer should obey God as set forth in His Word* (vv. 12, 16, 17). That King under whom the believer is a subject, to Him he should give obedience. He should hear His word of command and follow it. Obedience gives the clear evidence to whom one owes his allegiance. If one bows the knee in obedience to sin, it is clear that he is the servant of sin. If he bows the knee in obedience to God, it is clear that he is the servant of God (v. 16). Men who have heard the word of truth in the gospel and have obeyed that message from the heart are the servants of God and are justified. They should now obey the voice of God in the way they walk. That is the way of holiness and the answer to the problem of sin (John 17:17; 15:3; Eph. 5:26; I Peter 1:22).

3. *The pattern of life for the believer* (v. 14). The foregoing argument is based on the premise that believers are justified and stand in relation to God as righteous people. By identification with Christ in death they were cut off from sin, and therefore sin shall not be able to exercise lordship over them (v. 14a). And this fact that they have been translated into a new kingdom (Col. 1:13) grows out of the more basic fact that in the exercise of grace toward believers they are now no longer under law, but under grace. This not only describes the pattern of life for believers, but it also voices a promise for the next problem confronting the believer.

B. The justified man cannot indulge in the act of sin because of his identification with Christ (vv. 15-23). In the preceding section the apostle pointed out how the principle of union with Christ takes one out of the atmosphere and environment of sin.

But now he turns to the more practical issue of the actual committing of sin. That will explain the question with which this
portion begins. "What then? . . ." That is, where does that leave
us? What are the implications of the above argument? "Shall we
sin, because we are not under the law, but under grace?" Let us
scrutinize this matter more closely.

1. *The problem of particular sins* (v. 15). Though the general
area of sin in relation to the believer is still under consideration,
there is a shift to a particular aspect of sin. The question in verse
1 was, "Shall we continue *in* sin?" The problem had to do with
the permanent aspect of sin. But now the quesiton is, "Shall we
continue *to* sin?" The problem now is concerned with the particular act of sin. The argument of the apostle in dealing with the
first question was to show that the justified believer will not be
able to continue the life of sin. In the second question he has to
show that the believer will not even commit a single act of sin.[4]

Just as the apostle responded with an indignant negative,
"God forbid . . ." to the first proposal, so he responds in the same
way to the second; but this time for a different reason. In answer
to the first question Paul pointed out that being united with
Christ in death, burial, and resurrection places the believer in a
sphere where he cannot continue in sin. But now he will point
out that justified men have new motivations. Having a new
master, Christ, should therefore bring a fitting response. If one
sins he proves that Christ is not his master. A great saint was
known to say, "There is a subtle poison which insinuates itself
into the heart even of the best Christian; it is the temptation to
say: Let us sin not that grace may abound, but *because* it
abounds."[5]

2. *The pattern of personal allegiance* (vv. 16-18). Paul pays
deference to those to whom he is writing. He calls their attention
to the fact that they know perfectly well that the master they own

4. Thomas, *The Devotional Commentary: Romans Vol. II*, pp. 19-20.
5. F. Godet, *St. Paul's Epistle to the Romans* (Funk and Wagnalls: New
York, 1883), p. 253.

determines the allegiance they display. If sin is the master, then they will obey it; and if righteousness is the master, then they will obey righteousness. He is grateful to God that this group of believers made a choice, and the proof of that choice was that they obeyed from the heart a mold of doctrine constituting Christian truth. Within that mold they were taking on a new spiritual shape. Through this experience they were made free from sin and are now discharging the responsibilities of servants of righteousness. Serving a new master with a new voice and a new set of directions, they are now walking in the way of holiness.

3. *The performance of pure conduct* (vv. 19-20). Now the apostle addresses to them an appeal. It would appear that he puts that appeal into the form of social relations of that day. Perhaps some of these saints to whom he writes have been slaves or are even now slaves. In any event, slavery was a social form of the day. Just as they once bowed the knee to sin as their master and went from one degree of uncleanness and iniquity to a lower level, now that they have named Christ as their master they ought to present their members as servants to righteousness and move ever in the direction of holiness. When they were the servants of sin they were cut off from righteousness. So now being cut off from sin, let them serve Christ.

4. *The promise of eternal life* (vv. 21-23). What was the fruit of their past life and service? The end of these shameful things was death. But now joined to God as His servants, there is also fruit. It is always in the direction of holiness; and the end is a life like that of God, an everlasting life. The old life of sin paid wages. These wages were death. Under that regime a servant got what he deserved. But in the new kingdom, things are altogether different. What the believer has is a gift, a gift that is ministered through Jesus Christ our Lord. This is then an appeal addressed to a Christian and not a sinner. The wages of sin are earned and the worker has a right to demand his pay. But everlasting life is a gift to those who will accept it, and the only response can be a

life of gratitude. For such people, sinning becomes an absolute impossibility either as a course of life or as an indulgence of the moment. Identification with Christ in His death means cessation from sin. Identification with Christ in His resurrection means life and power for a new career.

II. THE PERILOUS ASPECTS OF SANCTIFICATION (7:1-25)

Fallen human nature follows one pattern—that is to depend on itself. Just as human nature sought to produce a righteousness which would be acceptable to God and failed, so also human nature seeks to generate holiness that will please God and will inevitably fail. The keeping of the law as the solution to the issues of life is inextricably joined with sinful human nature. The law gives the knowledge of sin (3:20), demonstrates the exceeding sinfulness of sin (7:13), provides an occasion for sin (7:8), and works wrath upon sin (4:15). But law has never provided righteousness for men, nor is it able to produce holiness in men. So lest justified men deliberately or unconsciously follow this perilous path, the argument of chapter 7 is introduced into the discussion.

In verse 14 of the preceding chapter a principle was enunciated to help the justified man confront the act of sin. "For sin shall not have dominion over you: for ye are not under law, but under grace." In the remainder of chapter 6 the apostle made clear what he meant by "ye are . . . under grace." It is now up to him to make equally clear what he meant by "ye are not under law." This becomes the subject and discussion of chapter 7. Already the apostle has touched upon law in relation to justification (3:20), law in relation to sin (5:20), and law in relation to believers (6:14). But each of these must be given further elaboration. They are treated in reverse order in chapter 7.[6]

A. Law and the Christian (vv. 1-6). The movement of thought proceeds over a fourfold pattern.

6. Thomas, *The Devotional Commentary: Romans Vol. II*, p. 28.

1. *The principle of law is clearly stated in verse 1.* The law has dominion over a man as long as he lives. Any infraction of the law will bring the authorities running and the law will impose its penalty.

2. *The illustration of severance from the law is the well-known law pertaining to marriage* (vv. 2-3). The law binds a woman to one man till death separates them. Any failure on the part of the woman to observe this law incriminates the woman. But if the man dies, the woman is set free from that law so that she is free to marry another man without stigma.

3. *The application to the believer is made immediately* (vv. 4-5). Before conversion the believer was subject to the law. But at conversion he identified himself with Christ in death, and this severed his connection with the law. Rising with Christ as a new man he could then be joined to Christ with no further control by the law. In this new relation he could bring forth fruit to God, whereas before in connection with the law the motions of sin brought forth fruit to death.

4. *The realization of new life and holiness develops from this new relationship* (v. 6). The old nature has now been rendered inoperative in relation to the law by death with Christ. So that now in this new state of freedom we may serve God in newness of spirit and not in oldness of letter. The new service is not like that of a slave to his master, but like that of a wife to her husband.

B. The law and sin emphasize the fact that the two operate together (vv. 7-13). A whole series of things marks the function of law in relation to sin.[7]

1. *The law unveils the fact of sin* (v. 7). The law is not sin. But it performs a special function assigned to it by the Lord. Though in early life one may be completely oblivious to sin, there comes a time when examining the law suddenly confronts one with the

7. Thomas, pp. 36-38.

fact of sin. When it says, "Thou shalt not covet," at that moment the sin of unholy desire is identified.

2. *The law provides the occasion for sin* (v. 8). The moment the law sets bounds for action the old nature is aroused and uses the law as an occasion to do what is forbidden.

3. *The law exposes the power of sin* (vv. 9-10). Living in complacency and joy is ended the moment the law confronts one; then the old sinful nature becomes active, and the law takes its toll and brings death.

4. *The law excites the deceitfulness of sin* (v. 11). The law creates in the sinful nature the false conception that the old nature can meet the law's demands, only to discover when it is too late that this was an outrageous deception.

5. *The law exhibits the sinfulness of sin* (vv. 12-13). The law is holy, and just, and good in spite of the fact that in its function it performs all of the above things. It is holy because it measures sin; it is just in that it calls for penalty upon sin; it is good because of its inherent nature and purpose. It is not the law that produces sin. It only provides the occasion for it. And it is not the law that brings death. It is sin that brings death. But by making sin exceedingly sinful, it also serves as a conductor to bring a hopeless sinner to Christ (Gal. 3:24).

C. The law and the carnal man is now treated in the final movement of thought in this chapter (vv. 14-25). In this passage the apostle is going to show the power of the sinful nature. Herein is demonstrated "what the law could not do, in that it was weak through the flesh" (8:3). Because of the weakness of the flesh the law could not justify (3:20); now additional truth is pointed out, namely, that it cannot sanctify.

Within this passage there are three cycles of confession. The first is recorded in verses 14-17; the second in verses 18-20; and the third in verses 21-25. Three elements characterize each cycle. There is a statement of fact, then a proof of the fact, and finally the conclusion. The statement in the first cycle is that he is carnal, sold under sin (v. 14). The statement of fact in the second is that in him dwelleth no good thing (v. 18). In the third cycle the statement of fact is that there is a law in him, ". . . evil is present with me" (v. 21).

In each cycle the proof of the fact is a conflict within. He recognizes the good or evil and approves or disapproves, but is unable to carry out his evaluation (vv. 15-16; 18b-19; 22-23). The conclusion in each case is also the same. It is no longer I that do it, but sin that dwelleth in me (vv. 17, 20, 24). In the third cycle the conclusion ends in a cry of anguish, a piercing cry of utter hopelessness and despair. "O wretched man that I am! who shall deliver me from the body of this death?" (v. 24).

In this moment of despair, when the sinful self has come to the end of itself and faces squarely up to the hopelessness of the situation, the light breaks through and the glad thanksgiving for deliverance in Christ breaks forth. "I thank God through Jesus Christ our Lord. . . ."

Enough of the original image of God remains that "the mind" recognizes the law of God and approves its moral evaluations. But there is so little of that original image remaining, now that the sinful flesh has taken over, that the flesh directs the course of life down the path marked out by the law of sin. The dismal and dreary discussion of this chapter should be enough to warn the believer away from the law as the pathway to holiness. It should send him back to chapter 6 and identification with Christ by faith. "Stand fast therefore in the liberty wherewith Christ hath made us free, and be not entangled again with the yoke of bondage" (Gal. 5:1).

Questions for Individual Study

1. What transition is made in the movement of thought from chapter 5 to chapter 6? What is the theme of chapter 6?
2. What two aspects of sin is the apostle attempting to deal with in the life of the believer?
3. What is meant by identification with Christ by faith? What does the believer experience?

4. What four words in the text aptly unfold the method of sanctification for the believer?
5. Why is it necessary for Paul to include the discussion of chapter 7?
6. What various things does the law do in relation to sin?
7. What is the nature of the conflict in the man who is trying to live by the law?

Chapter 6

Preservation and Its Final Triumph

Romans 8:1-39

Chapter 8 of Romans is the crowning argument in the explanation of the salvation that is in Christ Jesus our Lord. As expressed in the remarks of one expositor:

> In this surpassing chapter the several streams of the preceding arguments meet and flow in one "river of the water of life, clear as crystal, proceeding out of the throne of God and of the Lamb," until it seems to lose itself in the ocean of a blissful eternity. (Quoted from *Handbooks for Bible Classes: Romans,* by Dr. David Brown, p. 77)[1]

In this chapter the justification described in 3:21—5:21 and the sanctification elaborated in chapters 6 and 7 reach their culmination: "There is therefore now no condemnation to them which are in Christ Jesus" (8:1). That conclusion is the solid foundation upon which the argument of chapter 8 builds its superstructure of security and assurance. The argument mounts upward, level by level, with ever-advancing triumph until it reaches the capstone of no separation from the love of God in Christ Jesus our Lord (v. 39).

The justification and sanctification of the preceding chapters trace their source to union with Christ and erect their achievements on that firm foundation. Chapter 6 shows how utterly impossible it is for union with Christ to make provision for union with sin. And chapter 7 demonstrates how impossible it is for union with Christ to join in union with law. Thus far the reader has been thoroughly convinced of the exceeding sin-

---

1. W. H. Griffith Thomas, *The Devotional Commentary: Romans Vol. II,* p. 55.

fulness of sin (7:13) and servitude to the oldness of the letter (7:6).

Now is the time for describing a life patterned over the new-ness of spirit (7:6). The believer will now learn that the law is not merely God's requirement for holiness, but that it is also God's will for us in union with Christ. In the oldness of the letter the law first required strict adherence before it offered salvation. But in newness of spirit grace first gives before it makes any requirements. Therein lies victory. "For what the law could not do, in that it was weak through the flesh, God sending his own Son in the likeness of sinful flesh, and for sin, condemned sin in the flesh: that the righteousness of the law might be fulfilled in us, who walk not after the flesh, but after the Spirit" (8:3-4).

In fact, the grace that is in Christ Jesus goes even a step beyond this. In bringing the believer to realization of God's will as set forth in the righteousness of the law, it not only makes no demand upon the believer, but instead of that it imparts the desire to the believer to walk in the way of righteousness, so that the believer is no longer under bondage: "For it is God which worketh in you both to will and to do of his good pleasure" (Phil. 2:13). From the opening verse of chapter 8 to its close there is an ever-widening river of grace that finally culminates in absolute assurance of grand consummation.

The citadel of safety and assurance is presented in the opening verse of this chapter. It is "in Christ Jesus" (v. 1). Within the walls of this fortress there unfolds every facet of the faith as it bears upon the salvation of the believer from the moment of faith until the hour of glorification. And as the believer reaches the conclusion of his pilgrimage through life he is still within the fortress where there is no separation (v. 39).

There is no division of this chapter that is quite satisfying. Any division will be made over a pattern of human comprehension that is limited in vision, and therefore some of the truth will be overlooked. So it behooves the student to read the chapter over and over again. Flashes of truth that have not been seen before will emerge with each reading and bring blessing to the heart just as God intended. In all of it you cannot help but see that it begins with no condemnation and arrives at the blessed goal of no separation, and the reason lies in the fact that there is no defeat in between. Consider the following division as being at least helpful.

A. There is a new standing of the believer before God (vv. 1-4). The opening statement of the chapter (v. 1) is an announcement of this new standing. "There is therefore now no condemnation to them that are in Christ Jesus." "In Christ Jesus" constitutes a perfect standing. It is the same standing as that possessed by Christ Jesus. This standing means that the believer by faith has appropriated the righteousness provided by Christ in the work of the cross, so that the penalty for sin is fully paid, and the position he now occupies is that of a righteous person before God. Not even one little bit of condemnation remains for the believer to face. This is emphasized by the very first word of the Greek text, which loses some of its force in the English translations by the word "no." In Christ Jesus there remains not only not any condemnation resting on the believer, but also no legal burden of any kind, no disability or handicap for living a life of righteousness.[2]

The *perfect explanation* for this amazing fact is stated in verse 2. Though the latter half of verse 1 may have some value as a point of identification, the better manuscripts do not carry it. On the whole it seems out of place in the light of the context. But it is in place at the end of verse 4 and fits in properly with the movement of thought. Thus, the explanation for the statement in verse 1 follows immediately in verse 2, "For the law of the Spirit of life in Christ Jesus hath made me free from the law of sin and death." Herein is the reason why there is no condemnation. Union with Christ brings the believer into vital relation to a new power, the rule of the Holy Spirit. The Spirit gives life, and life that is infinite in power and is able to control the sinful nature. This means that the believer is delivered from the law of sin and

2. Thomas, p. 66.

death. This is that resurrection power ministered to us by the Spirit (Eph. 1:19-20), which consists of "newness of life" (6:4) and "newness of spirit" (7:6).

The *divine method* in accomplishing this feat is expressed in verse 3. The law had no power to condemn sin in our flesh so as to bring its activity to an end. Nor did it have any power to produce righteous conformity to its standards. The reason lay in the weakness of the flesh. There was nothing in the flesh to bring an effective response. But God had the necessary power to effect a solution. It is entirely supernatural. The eternal Father caused His eternal Son to become incarnate in human flesh, sin apart, and He condemned sin in the flesh by first making full atonement for sin. This broke the rule of sin and death. This death consisted of propitiation, expiation, and redemption from the penalty and power of sin (3:21-26). Identification with Christ by faith makes all this effective in the believer (6:3-5).

The *essential purpose* of this divine operation is clearly explained in verse 4. This purpose has intimate relation to the law. The law of God is holy, just, good, and spiritual (7:12, 14), and expresses the will of God for the lives of His children. It is not to be lightly esteemed or ignored. Nor is it to be used in such a way that it fails to fulfill God's purpose. Therefore God opened up the way for its accomplishment in the lives of His own by a walk which is characterized in every aspect by the Spirit of God. This walk covers the entire routine of life and traces its energy to the power of the Holy Spirit. The law is spiritual in the sense that the Spirit is its author and promoter. When the Spirit works in a life He promotes the righteousness of the law so that it characterizes that life. That is the remarkable achievement of the plan of God in salvation.

B. There is a new standard of measure for evaluation (vv. 5-8). In the preceding verses (vv. 1-4) Paul has demonstrated that only justified men can be holy. In this passage he will point up the fact that only holy men are justified.

The *rule of measure* is set forth in the word "after," used in verses 4 and 5. It renders a Greek preposition meaning "as measured by." For evaluating men in their relationship to God there is one rule—as measured by the flesh, and another—as measured by the Spirit. This covers the wide spectrum of the entire life: motivation, thoughts, words, and deeds. That which is according to or measured by the flesh will include everything proceeding from the old, sinful, unregenerate nature. It points to the entire life lived apart from God. It may include that which is low, gross, and vicious, but not necessarily so. It may be marked by that which is literate, cultured, refined, and altruistic. It even includes that which is religious, sometimes to the point of fanaticism in the area of outward ceremonies and rites, asceticism, and self-sacrifice. Still, there is nothing about it that is acceptable with God.

On the other hand, that which is measured by the Spirit is that which proceeds from the Spirit of God and in every detail and aspect meets with the approval of God. Such who live this life are the kind of people who have been justified by faith, who have been born of the Spirit, and who walk according to the Spirit. They are the absolute opposite of those "after the flesh." These two kinds of men are mutually separated. They are clearly recognizable as belonging to two different classes. The one is justified and sanctified. The other is unjustified and unholy.

The *controlling mind* of these two classes is also set in clear distinction in verses 6 and 7. The word "mind" refers to that controlling principle in each. It points to understanding, comprehension, concern, prudence, and ambition. The "mind of the flesh" is the product of the flesh. Its understanding of reality, comprehension of God, and ruling principle are conditioned entirely by the sinful nature, designed to give expression to the sinful nature, and directed to the end of accomplishing the purposes of the sinful nature. But "the mind of the Spirit" is wholly the product of the Spirit of God.

The *essential meaning* of these two minds provides a picture marked by clear contrasts. The mind of the flesh is marked by hostility toward God. It is the enemy of God. It is also marked by insurgency. It is insubordinate toward God. It will not bow the knee in subjection to His law. It is also characterized by inability to keep the law of God. No matter what pretenses to the contrary, it is thoroughly incapable of keeping God's law. And finally it is marked by futility. Its destined end is death, that is, the abrogation of all that is good, and holy, and worthwhile. All of its efforts will come to nothing.

What profound contrast there is in meaning in "the mind of the Spirit." As over against hostility there is peace, tranquility; as over against insubordination there is subjection; as over against inability there is power; as over against futility in death there is life, everlasting life. There is everything that will please God and bring His approval.

C. There is a new energizing power for living (vv. 9-11). This is the Spirit of God. Those who live in the sphere of the flesh do not have the Spirit of God. If they do not have the Spirit of God, they do not belong to Christ. But those to whom he writes are clearly regarded as those who are not in the flesh, but are in the Spirit. They do possess the Spirit of God and therefore they do belong to God and are capable of living a life for God.

This means that *something has happened* to them that differentiates them from what they were before they came to Christ. When the Spirit of God dwells in the believer, the body is dead because of sin. He means to say that association with Adam physically does not immediately change, and he will be subject to physical death. But the human spirit has been made alive because of the righteousness into which he entered by faith, for the Spirit of God has come to dwell in the human spirit (see verse 10 in ASV and NIV).

Something will yet happen to the believer that should encourage him (v. 11). Even though the body is destined for physical death because of sin in relation to the first Adam, the presence of the Spirit of God gives promise that even in death there will be a quickening of the body of the saint and he will experience resurrection just as in the case of Christ. In the plan of God there are measured developments as He sees fit. Even though the Spirit of God comes in at conversion to dwell in the believer, that does not mean that all the benefits of salvation are to be realized at the same time. There is one that is reserved for the future, namely, bodily resurrection. But the withholding of that blessing from immediate experience does not argue that the first fruits of the Spirit have not been received. Let the saint take courage even in the face of persecution and possible death. Let him live for Christ now no matter what the cost, for there will be a physical resurrection (I Cor. 15:58).

D. There is a new family relationship as a result of conversion (vv. 12-17). Certain things come with this new relationship.

1. *There is the obligation to live like members of the family* (vv. 12-13). The flesh has never made any contribution to the believer, so there is no moral obligation to live after the flesh. The obligation is in the opposite direction. Living after the flesh demonstrates that one does not belong to the family of God, and such a course of life will end in death. But if one makes it a habit to put to death the deeds of the flesh by means of the Spirit, this is a clear token that he will live. It is clear evidence that he is living spiritually now, and that he will someday live physically.

The believer cannot put to death the old nature, but he can make inactive the deeds of the body that give expression to the old nature. This may be done by means of the Spirit. It is much like the little girl who declared that Paul kept under his body by keeping his soul on top. Giving priority to the Spirit of God will accomplish this.

2. *There are certain privileges that come to members of the family* (vv. 14-15). Being led by the Spirit of God is evidence that one occupies the position of a son. It is evidence that he has been elevated to the position of sonship with certain rights and privileges. He has been transferred from one family to the family of God by official action; but more than that, the proof of that is that the Spirit of God has taken up His residence in the son so that he also shares the nature of the family. He is not a poor relation or a slave who is in bondage to a master; but he is a son, standing on the same level with every other member of the family, and as a child, cries out, "Abba, Father," just as Christ did in the garden (Mark 14:36).

3. There is also mutual testimony to the Father that they are children of God (vv. 16-17). This is Paul's way of saying that the Spirit of God and the spirit of the saint make a common testimony to the heavenly Father that the believer is a child of God. This does not mean that the Spirit bears testimony to our spirit, but that with our spirit both bear testimony to God. Our spirits look up and call God Father, and the Spirit of God joins with us and bears the same testimony. This double testimony is no mere flash of sentiment, but a witness to a fact apart from any emotion, a certainty that gives unalterable assurance of relation and destiny. This destiny includes inheritance, an inheritance equal to that of Christ since both are joint heirs. Present experience of suffering with Christ clearly points to future glorification together.

E. There is a new expectation for the future (vv. 18-25). Reference to inheritance and being glorified with Christ encourages Paul to add a new feature for the comfort of the saints.

1. Present sufferings are not the final stage of Christian experience (v. 18). Christians of that day and since have been subjected to suffering in varying degrees. But the future holds a glory to be revealed in believers that far outweighs present suffering, and it will last forever.

2. Irrational creation looks forward to that grand climax (vv. 19-22). When men fell into sin, the creation too suffered some change from its original constitution. A curse fell on it so that in the cycles of change there is a sort of uselessness, a failure to accomplish a reasonable purpose. Someday, when there comes the manifestation of the sons of God, creation itself will enter into the results. Catastrophes and cataclysms will cease. Drought and flood and desert and cold will disappear.

3. Further confirmation of coming glory is cherished by the saints themselves (v. 23). They now have the first fruits in the possession of the Spirit. But they look forward with earnest longing for the completion of salvation. This will include the

raising and changing of the body, so that it will be like the body of His glory (Phil. 3:20-21).

4. *Eager persistence is generated by the hope we have in the future* (vv. 24-25). Hope is never concerned with the present. Hope is the expectation of some future reality that has not yet been experienced. It is that expectation of the future goal that keeps us determined to go on in the direction to reach that goal. As a result it produces a patience in us, a dogged determination to withstand all the opposition and penetrate through all the obstacles that we may finally arrive at the goal. We wait for it in the sense that there is an eagerness that constantly characterizes our determination. We do not sorrow over our present plight, for there is something better ahead.

F. There is a new assistance for personal achievement (vv. 26-27). In this case it is divine assistance. And it is so needed. Christians are pilgrims making a journey to the future. Because they do not know what lies ahead they are constantly praying for God to provide those necessary things to meet the problems of the way. Unfortunately they do not know what they ought to pray for. But there is a divine helper, the Holy Spirit of God. He not only knows the needs, but He also knows the will of God, and He prays for us. He makes no mistakes. What we need we get and therefore can be assured that we can make the journey to its end without fail.

G. There is a new comprehension of the program of God (vv. 28-30). The believer now has an overall view of the plan of God as it relates to himself. That plan reaches from eternity to eternity. Before the world was, God foreknew and predestinated us to be His children and to be conformed to the image of His Son. There came a day when the gospel reached us and we believed it and were justified. His plan is so certain that He has already glorified us. But to provide the means to the end He spans the intervening gap between faith and glory by causing everything to work together for good. Our evaluation of things along the way is given in terms of good and bad, but by His mighty power and wisdom He takes every one of them and works them for good in such a way that at last we will be completely conformed to the image of His Son.

H. There is a new certainty of the final triumph (vv. 31-39). "What shall we then say to these things?" What things? The things that have been discussed in chapters 3 through 8—the things that have to do with our justification, sanctification, and preservation. Paul responds without hesitation or fear with three things:

1. *The relation of these things to God* (vv. 31b-33). God is for us. Everything in the preceding argument describes what God has done and is doing for us. No one can be against us. Who could? No one can stand up against God, and since God is on our side that is all that matters. In our behalf He did not spare His own Son. But more than that, He has given to us His Son, and with His Son comes everything. Who is there that has a right to lay a charge against us? The one and only judge is God, and in place of condemning us, He justifies us.

2. *The relation of these things to Christ* (v. 34). Who is it that has the right to condemn us? Christ is the only one, but He moved in a different direction. He died for us. He rose again to prove that He had cleared the scroll of any indictment. He ascended to the right hand of the Father where He exercises advocacy on our behalf (I John 2:2). There in heaven He serves as our intercessor and high priest in a ministry that saves to the uttermost (Heb. 7:24-25). Undergirded with this perfect provision there can be no possible condemnation. In all this Christ is set forth as our "righteousness, and sanctification, and redemption" (I Cor. 1:30).

3. *The relation of the circumstances of creation* (vv. 35-39). Is there anyone or anything that is sufficient to separate believers from the love of Christ? He then begins to name the various areas of pressure and the circumstances that might be suggested. But he is convinced there is none. Even though the saints have

suffered in other days and still suffer, without protest they still march to the slaughter like sheep (Ps. 44:22). But in the face of that they are conquerors and beyond. They not only face the perils and pressures, but through these they are brought on their way toward the goal. It has brought them to the perfect persuasion expressed by Paul that there is nothing capable in the area of creation of separating them from the love of God which is in Christ Jesus our Lord.[3]

Spurgeon once saw on a weathercock the words, "God is love," whereupon he remarked to his companion that he did not think this was appropriate on so changeable a thing. But he was met with the answer that he had misinterpreted the meaning. What it really meant was that "God is love" no matter which way the wind blows.

Questions for Individual Study

1. What place does the teaching of the eighth chapter of Romans occupy in relation to the entire discussion on salvation?
2. What does the new standing mean to the believer as set forth in chapter 8 and verse 1?
3. What does Paul mean by the expressions: "after the flesh" and "after the Spirit"?
4. What is the new energizing power by which the believer is enabled to live a holy life?
5. Where does hope enter into the experience of the believer to encourage him on to the outcome?
6. What new assistance is given to the believer to assure him of making a successful journey?
7. What are some of the things that lead the apostle Paul to the conclusion that the salvation of the believer is certain?

3. G. Campbell Morgan, Searchlights from the Word (Charles Higham and Son, Ltd.: London, 1946), p. 335.

Chapter 7

The Sovereign Election of Israel to Favor

Romans 9:1-33

The eighth chapter of Romans ended with a note of triumph. The people of God are conquerors. They are more than conquerors. There is no realm of existence, whether it be death or life; there is no echelon of intelligent beings, whether angels, or principalities, or powers; there is no expanse of time filled with things, whether present or future; there is no level of creation, whether height reaching to heaven or depth descending to hell; nor is there any other creation that can storm the citadel of the saint and separate him from the love of God in Christ Jesus our Lord.

But that note of ecstasy is suddenly lost in the sorrow expressed by the apostle for his people in the opening words of chapter 9. However, this is not out of character. In fact, it marks the close psychological relation to the preceding chapter.[1] Here is a heart that is heavily burdened for the spiritual condition of his own countrymen. Is this not the natural response of a heart that has been brought into vital communion with the Savior? Paul's first concern is for those loved ones who yet wander in darkness and sin. He is so deeply concerned for the spiritual welfare of his people that if it were possible he would endure the wrath of God upon himself for their sakes. This is similar to the selfless devotion of the great leader Moses, who, in the wilderness, asked God to blot him from the book of life for the sake of his people (Exod. 32:32).[2] Paul and Moses demonstrated how

---

1. W. H. Griffith Thomas, *The Devotional Commentary: Romans Vol. II*, p. 112.
2. J. Agar Beet, *St. Paul's Epistle to the Romans*, p. 252.

intimately they shared in the mind of Christ, who also lamented over his people:

> O Jerusalem, Jerusalem, thou that killest the prophets, and stonest them which are sent unto thee, how often would I have gathered thy children together, even as a hen gathereth her chickens under her wings, and ye would not! Behold, your house is left unto you desolate. For I say unto you, Ye shall not see me henceforth, till ye shall say, Blessed is he that cometh in the name of the Lord (Matt. 23:37-39).

And Christ did what neither Paul nor Moses could do. He actually took their punishment. He substituted in their place (Gal. 3:13; Isa. 53:6; Matt. 27:46).

For those who have not caught the deep devotion of the apostle and his intimate identification with the theme he is unfolding, there may seem to be a hiatus in the argument.[3] To them it would seem that he should have moved immediately to the hortatory section of chapter 12. This would be in harmony with the pattern of development in other epistles. After unfolding the doctrine he always moved into the application to duty. That leads those who move on the surface in their interpretation of Romans to believe that the apostle has introduced a parenthetical section that has no intimate logical relation to the main movement of thought.

However, that explanation misses the underlying connections, such connections that make it clear that the apostle is not through with the doctrinal elaboration of the gospel. How could the apostle strike so heavily upon the theme that there is no separation from the love of God (8:39) and not think of God's love in relation to his people? Paul knew that God set His love upon Israel for no virtue in themselves (Deut. 7:7-8). He knew that in those dark days of the Northern Kingdom, through Hosea, He had declared, "I will heal their backsliding, I will love them freely: for mine anger is turned away from him" (14:4). He could not forget when at last God had turned the Southern Kingdom over to Babylon for destruction that through Jeremiah He had

3. F. F. Bruce, *The Epistle of Paul to the Romans*, p. 181.

said, "Yea, I have loved thee with an everlasting love: therefore with lovingkindness have I drawn thee" (31:3). How is love from which there is no separation to be reconciled with the condition of his people Israel, which as a nation is in rebellion against God and repudiation of Christ?

Did not the gospel come first to the Jew (Rom. 1:16)? Was not the early church made up completely of Jews (Acts 2:5, 22, 41)? But after the first great swell of enthusiasm for the gospel in Jewry, did there not break out a persecution against the church, and the gospel, and Christ, led by a Pharisee by the name of Paul (Acts 4:1-2; 8:1-4)? From this point on did not the other apostles as well as Paul himself encounter such bitter opposition from the Jews that it was necessary to turn to the Gentiles (Acts 13:16-47; 18:6; 28:24-28)? In the light of this would not the Jewish segment of the church raise some insuperable problems about the power of the gospel and the reliableness of God's promises to His people Israel? If Jewish Christians are to be put at rest some of these problems must be resolved. That is in part why this section must appear at this point in the epistle.[4]

But the matter does not end with the Jewish Christian. There is also the Gentile believer. The only Scriptures he knows anything about are Jewish Scriptures. The Old Testament was the Bible of the early church. The Gentile believer could not fail to recognize the promises and prophecies made to the nation of Israel. If those promises to Israel have failed, what assurance is there that promises made to believers in the gospel have any more validity? Can the promises in the gospel be trusted? Just because Paul can conclude with a crescendo of praise and assurance as to the security of the believer as set forth in Romans 8, is that to be taken as genuine or just a mere burst of emotion? Paul knows perfectly well that this too must be handled if this great argument he has just concluded is to be accepted at face value.

Above all else, there needs to be clearly demonstrated that the

---

4. Alva J. McClain, The Jewish Problem and Its Divine Solution (The Brethren Missionary Herald Company: Winona Lake, 1944), p. 5.

gospel which Paul preached was no mere innovation.[5] Beginning with the Protevangelium, the first gospel intended for the
entire human race (Gen. 3:15), the development and fulfillment
were deeply rooted in history, and especially with the history of
a particular nation. It was initiated by promise to Abraham (Gen.
12:1-3), and further "promised afore by his prophets in the holy
scriptures" (Rom. 1:2). Its subject matter was God's Son, "which
was made of the seed of David according to the flesh" (1:3). This
means that the gospel was inseparably associated with the nation of Israel, so much so that it is affirmed that "salvation is of
the Jews" (John 4:22). The Messiah of the gospel was to come
and save Israel and give Israel a rightful priority among the
nations (Deut. 28:1, 13). Viewing the situation at hand, any
thinking individual would be apt to ask the serious question
whether Christ was the true Messiah. For it was preeminently
the descendants of Abraham who refused to accept Him and
believe the gospel. Either this Jesus is not the promised Messiah,
or else the promises to Israel have failed. This theological di-
lemma must be resolved, and this is the point in the epistle
where this discussion should appear.

In some respects these three chapters constitute the most
important portion of the entire epistle. The gospel stands or falls
on the resolution of the problem now to be discussed. The
movement of thought is logical and progressive. In chapter 9 the
present situation of Israel is evaluated from the standpoint of
divine sovereignty. In chapter 10 the situation in Israel is measured over against human responsibility. Chapter 11 is an effort
to bring these two lines of truth into conformity with the overall
final and saving purpose of God. At this point we will examine
the reasoning of Paul as set forth in chapter 9.

I. INTRODUCTION TO THE PROBLEM OF ISRAEL (9:1-5)

**A. The solemn concern of the apostle is indicated by his
method of making approach to the problem relating to his**

5. Bruce, *The Epistle of Paul to the Romans*, p. 183.

people (vv. 1-2). He brings to bear a threefold certification of the situation: "in Christ," "conscience," and "the Holy Spirit."[6] On the positive side this is *the truth*, the outline of which he has discussed in the first eight chapters of the book. This leaves the Jews under the penalty of wrath. But it also opens up the way of life to them in the gospel. On the negative side it is *no lie*. What he is about to unfold is no fabrication developed out of a tissue of unreality. Moreover, objective truth on the one hand and subjective operation of the Spirit on the other join in bearing witness in his conscience. The intense feeling of sorrow on the part of the apostle grows out of fact in relation to his people.

B. The serious condition is marked by the fact that the apostle could wish that he were anathema from Christ for the sake of his people (v. 3). So closely is the apostle identified with his people that their desperate condition drives him to this wish. When Moses of old became aware of the awful sin into which his people had fallen, he, like Paul, would gladly have suffered in their stead (Exod. 32:32). But this was denied to each of them. In fact, it would have been impossible. But their desire demonstrated how intimately they shared in the mind of Christ. Like no other, Christ identified Himself with His people and sorrowed for them (Matt. 23:37-39; Luke 19:41-44), and He did suffer in their stead (Isa. 53:1-6; Gal. 3:13).

C. But the sovereign choice of Israel as a nation remains an eternal fact which the apostle now affirms as a present reality (vv. 4-5). Consider the amazing collection of blessings to Israel.

1. Position and privilege are given to Israel. They are Israelites and therefore princes with God (Gen. 32:28), being granted privileges that belong only to adopted sons (Exod. 4:22; Hos. 1:10; 11:1).

2. The presence of God became a reality with this people never granted to any other. The Shekinah glory took up residence in

---

6. A. T. Robertson, *Word Pictures in the New Testament*, p. 380.

the tabernacle and later in the temple (Exod. 40:34; I Kings 8:10 f.).

3. *The promises of God made in unconditional covenants to Abraham and successively to the people were granted to them* (Gen. 12:1-3; 13:14-17; 15:4-6, 18; 17:4-8; Exod. 24:8; 34:10; Jer. 31:31-34).

4. *The precepts of God in the giving of the law were made to Israel to serve as protection for them and as a child leader to bring them finally to Christ* (Exod. 20; Gal. 3:24).

5. *The prescriptions of God for divine service were given to them.* This was the God-given religion of Judaism as set forth in the Books of Exodus and Leviticus. All of this was an object lesson of provision finally made for them in Christ (Heb. 9:1 ff.).

6. *The prophecies and promises of God pointing forward to the coming of the Messiah were also a part of that grand contribution made to Israel* (Isa. 7:14; 9:6-7; 53; 55:1-4; Acts 13:23, 32-34).

7. *The patriarchs of Israel to whom these promises were made were also in that line of gifts to Israel.* These promises began with Abraham, were renewed to Isaac, and then were also made to Jacob and his sons (Gen. 12:1-3; 26:1-5; 28:11-15; 49; Lev. 26:42-45).

8. *The person of Christ is the climax and consummation of the exaltation given to Israel.* On the human side He came through the fathers, but on the divine side He is God. "God blessed forever" is an affirmation of fact and not an ascription of praise.[7]

II. THE OPERATION OF DIVINE ELECTION (9:6-13)

Up to this point in the chapter Paul has been discussing national favor with God. It is this fact that provides the basis for the resolution of the problem concerning Israel which he will

7. Bruce, *The Epistle of Paul to the Romans*, p. 186.

state clearly and concisely in 11:29. If he had been discussing individual salvation there would have been nothing more to say. For the rank and file of Israel at this time was in unbelief and therefore lost. On the human side they had frustrated the purpose of God in Christ.

A. The statement of relationship is the thing that establishes the truth of the word of God (vv. 6-7). God's Word never fails. But to understand what that means the explanation must be sought of God. Not everyone who traces his physical lineage to Israel is counted as being a member of the nation of Israel as God looks at it. A case in point is Ishmael and Isaac. While it is true that on the physical side both Isaac and Ishmael were children of Abraham, yet as God accounts true relationship Isaac alone was the seed of Abraham. For he was not only the son of promise, but he was in fact the son whom God by a singular act of divine power caused to be born (4:19).

B. The selection of children in the line of Abraham establishes the point Paul is making (vv. 8-11a). Isaac and Jacob were not children of the flesh; that is, they were not generated by human planning and effort. They were children of promise and apart from human works. Abraham and Sarah were helpless to generate a child but God gave them one. Jacob was selected while in the womb of his mother, so that works was excluded. The selection was by divine purpose and the fulfillment resided solely in Him who calls (Gen. 25:21-23). The same is true of Isaac.

C. The sovereignty of God is the absolute and final explanation for national favor (vv. 11b-13). God has a purpose which arises within Himself alone. It has no relation to men whether they do good or evil, and is therefore apart from works. No matter what the custom of that day, God had a right to determine that Esau, the elder, should serve Jacob, the younger. On the basis of that principle He had a perfect right to love Jacob and hate Esau (Mal. 1:2-3). This is what He did in relation to the nation of Israel. He determined to love this nation no matter how unlovely they were.

III. THE PRINCIPLE OF DIVINE ELECTION (9:14-18)

A. A searching question is introduced at this point which expresses precisely what is in the mind of most objectors: "Is there unrighteousness with God?" (v. 14). An affirmative answer to that question is unthinkable; but even so, it is raised. To this Paul responds with that absolute No, "God forbid." The question means this: If a man who is profligate is received on account of his faith, while a man who is outwardly moral is rejected because of unbelief, does that not suggest on the basis of appearance that there is injustice on the part of God? Clear understanding of the first eight chapters of this book forbids such an objection. But still, there are some who do raise this objection. To answer it, verses 15-18 are given.

B. The bestowal of mercy on the part of God forbids any such charge against God (vv. 15-16). When Israel fell into deep sin and deserved judgment, God bestowed mercy and declared to Moses His right to do so (Exod. 33:19). All Israel at this time was deserving of judgment and God was actually in the process of inflicting it. But then He decided to bestow mercy on some and save them. They did not deserve it. They did not call for it. They did not work for it. But God did exercise mercy. In judgment God caused three thousand to die for their indulgence in idolatry (Exod. 32:28), but the remainder of the people were extended mercy as a clear exhibition of God's sovereign goodness.

C. The infliction of judgment also falls into the same pattern of divine sovereignty (vv. 17-18). To highlight this point Paul uses the instance of Pharaoh. To him God did not extend mercy. Instead the Lord hardened him (Exod. 10:20). God permitted Pharaoh to harden his own heart toward Him, for it was His purpose to use this monarch as an occasion and center to demonstrate His power and identity (Exod. 7:3, 13, 14; 9:16). As evidence of this sovereign movement upon the king, over and over again Pharaoh hardened his heart (8:15, 19, 32; 9:34, 35). In His sovereignty God chose this king, who deserved judgment, as the special object for the display of His power (Exod. 9:12; 10:1, 20, 27; 14:4, 8, 17). If there is no unrighteousness with God in showing mercy, certainly there is no unrighteousness in His execution of judgment.

IV. THE CHARACTER OF SOVEREIGN ELECTION (9:19-24)

A. At this point a subtle insinuation is made by the objector to escape responsibility for sin (v. 19). If God is absolutely sovereign and everything obeys His will, then why should any fault be found against a man in sin? Is he not after all just what God made him? And if that be true, then the fault lies with God and not with the sinner. Obviously the person who does any thinking will recognize here a pattern of response which has been prevalent among men throughout all ages. When the issues of wrongdoing draw the noose more tightly about them, men squirm in an effort to escape; and they frequently try to shift the blame to someone else.

B. But Paul brings a striking indictment against the objector (vv. 20-21). It appears to him as sheer arrogance to reply against God in such fashion. Consider the potter as he works with the clay (Isa. 64:6-8). The thing that is being formed does not order the potter as to what sort of vessel it wants to be. But out of the same quality of material, from the same lump of clay, the potter makes a vessel to honor or to dishonor as it pleases him. By the same token all men are lost and deserve judgment. But God decided to save some and to permit others to suffer punishment.

C. It is important here to consider the saving inclination of the Lord in relation to all sinners (vv. 22-24). On the basis of God's justice He is ready and willing to pour out wrath upon sinners. But He has not done so. The reason lies in the fact that God is also a God of love and mercy, and His disposition is not toward judgment but toward salvation. God is not slack concerning His promise to men but is longsuffering (II Peter 3:9), not planning that any should perish, but that all should have plenty of time to repent. If any have been saved it is because they have had time to accept (II Peter 3:15). If any are lost it is because they have fitted themselves for destruction.[8] In this way it has been possible for God to pour out His blessing upon those who believe. And among them there are both Jews and Gentiles.

V. THE SCRIPTURAL PROOF FOR DIVINE ELECTION (9:25-20)

At this point the apostle cites a series of scriptures from the Old Testament to support the argument for election.

A. The quality of election is pointed out by reference to Hosea 2:22-23 (v. 25). Jewish people in the Northern Kingdom had apostatized from the Lord like an adulterous wife. But the love of the Lord was so strong toward them that He determined to show mercy in spite of what they deserved.

B. The breadth of election is suggested by Hosea 1:10 (v. 26). If this passage does not refer to Israel, then perhaps it reaches beyond Israel to the Gentiles. And undeserving though they may be, upon some of them God will set His sovereign love.

C. The limits of election are suggested by a quotation from Isaiah 10:22-23 (vv. 27-28). The natural seed of Israel may be like the sand of the sea for number, but only a remnant will be saved. God will choose that remnant and they will respond in faith to His call.

D. The depths of election are pointed out by another quotation from Isaiah 1:9 (v. 29). The wickedness of Israel was so great that all in Israel were deserving of a judgment like that which fell upon Sodom and Gomorrah. But in sovereign grace God moved upon them to save a remnant.

VI. THE CONCLUSION CONCERNING DIVINE ELECTION (9:30-33)

8. McClain, *The Jewish Problem and Its Divine Solution*, p. 14.

This portion of the chapter is at once a conclusion to the discussion on sovereign election and a transition to the theme of human responsibility to be discussed in the succeeding chapter. It is introduced by a question which calls for a conclusion. Note at least three things:

A. The success of the Gentiles is to be explained by the fact that they sought righteousness by faith (v. 30). As a people they did not follow after righteousness. The description has already been given in chapter 1. But when the truth of the gospel reached them and they recognized the righteousness of God that could be obtained by faith, they accepted it.

B. The failure of the Israelites is to be explained by the fact that even though they followed hard after righteousness in the law, this turned them away from the righteousness by faith, and so they did not attain to the law of righteousness (v. 31). That explains why the nation almost completely rejected the gospel.

C. The essential explanation for failure centers in their attitude toward Christ (vv. 32-33). Centuries before, Isaiah had prophesied what their response would be (8:14; 28:16). They would stumble over Christ. Disappointment in Him would lead them to reject Him. They did this deliberately. This is the stone to which Peter referred: rejected, yet elect, precious—precious to those who believe on Him, but a stone of stumbling to those who reject Him; and a stone who is made the head of the corner and will crush all those who are disobedient (I Peter 2:6-8).

Questions for Individual Study

1. What abrupt change in the temper of the apostle is to be noted in the transition from chapter 8 to chapter 9?
2. What two groups of people needed the explanation of chapters 9-11, and why?
3. What special blessings and privileges did God bestow on the nation of Israel?
4. How is election demonstrated in the history of Isaac and Ishmael, Esau and Jacob?
5. How does Paul illustrate the fact that God was not unrighteous in

election when he showed mercy to Israel and judged Pharaoh?
6. How does Paul meet the objection that since God is sovereign in election, the sinner is therefore not at fault for his sin?
7. Does Scripture support the doctrine of election? What do the Scriptures from Hosea and Isaiah mean?

Chapter 8

The Human Rejection of God's Provision
Romans 10:1-21

7-24-77

The formal argument defending the sovereignty of God in electing Israel to national favor is now concluded. The problem in relation to Israel was first clearly stated (9:1-5). The method of its operation was then described (9:6-13). The underlying principle of election was then pointed out (9:14-18). At this point the essential character of election was declared (9:19-24), and Scriptural proof was cited to undergird the argument (9:25-29). Finally, the conclusion was drawn, showing how election provides for the exercise of personal faith (9:30-33).

Now that the apostle has skillfully carried the argument forward to the place where human responsibility enters the picture, he pursues the element of human responsibility to its conclusion in chapter 10. "In this chapter the writer makes no attempt to soften or weaken that which he has written concerning God's sovereignty in the previous chapter."[1] "God is sovereign; as the Potter He has a right over the clay; He has mercy upon whom He will."[2] This is fundamental; for if there is salvation for anyone, it lies in the fact that God is sovereign, and in sovereign grace moves upon men to save them.

"But he will now show that no man can make even a sovereign God responsible for his sin and unbelief. The Jew alone is responsible for his lost condition."[3] It should therefore become

---

1. Alva J. McClain, *The Epistle to the Romans: Outlined and Summarized*, p. 35.
2. McClain, *The Jewish Problem and Its Divine Solution*, p. 17.
3. McClain, *The Epistle to the Romans: Outlined and Summarized*, p. 35.

apparent that "the ninth and tenth chapters of Romans should never be sundered in reading and study. They belong together, each presenting a distinctive aspect of a difficult problem. The ninth chapter explains why some Jews are saved. Chapter 10 explains why others are lost."[4]

The movement of thought in chapter 10 is fourfold. It opens with a section dealing with the responsibility of all (vv. 1-3). It proceeds by demonstrating the fact that there is accessibility of the gospel for all (vv. 4-10). It then makes perfectly clear that there is opportunity for all in that the only requirement is faith (vv. 11-15). In bringing the argument on human responsibility to its conclusion Paul asserts that the reason for failure was the inflexibility of the Jews toward the gospel (vv. 16-21).

I. THE RESPONSIBILITY OF ALL TO THE GOSPEL (10:1-3)

The approach of the apostle to the discussion on human responsibility is both personal and national. As for himself, the apostle is moved by an overpowering aspiration for the salvation of his people (v. 1). He is keenly aware of the fact that driving obsession characterizes their pattern of conduct (v. 2). Failure on their part must be traced to one thing—spiritual insubordination (v. 3).

A. Paul's personal aspiration for Israel is for their salvation (v. 1). The word "desire" is hardly strong enough to express precisely what Paul is trying to say. This word means "will," "pleasure," "satisfaction," perhaps all that is comprehended in the word *plan*. It is used that way of God in Philippians 2:13. Paul's great purpose is to see his kinsmen saved. So he does not miss one opportunity to reach them for Christ.

This purpose drives him to prayer, that is, the expression of petition in their behalf. The very fact that he goes to God seeking their salvation is proof that he recognizes the sovereignty of God, and realizes that any salvation comes from God in sovereign grace. This also means that he has not written his

4. McClain, *The Jewish Problem and Its Divine Solution*, p. 17.

people off as falling outside the possibility of salvation. It further means that he recognizes the place of human responsibility, that there is possibility for salvation to those who will respond in faith. So he prays to God that He will work in this people to exercise faith in the Lord Jesus Christ.

B. From its organization at Mount Sinai there has been national obsession for righteousness by works (v. 2). No one could speak more authoritatively on this point than Paul. Such persistent pursuit of righteousness through works had marked the course of his life until that day he met Christ on the Damascus road. During those early days under Gamaliel he outstripped his fellow students in zeal toward the traditions of his fathers (Gal. 1:13-14). It was this display of zeal that doubtless explains his progress in Jewry to the point where he became a member of the Sanhedrin. This became such a passion with him that he became the leader of the Sadducean persecution of the early church (Acts 4:1-4; 7:58; 8:1-3; 9:1 ff.). In reviewing his past life up to the point of conversion he makes special mention of this zeal, a zeal that was without knowledge (Phil. 3:5-6). All of this became clear to him that moment he met Christ on the Damascus road. Writing to the saints in Rome, Paul was acutely aware of the path his own countrymen were following. They possessed zeal but without knowledge, that is, without full knowledge, as the intensive form of the word means. They were zealous for the letter and the form, but the person and the spirit of their own scriptures escaped them.

C. This course of life resolved itself into spiritual insubordination (v. 3). In ignorance of God's righteousness, and exercising diligence to establish their own righteousness, they refused to submit themselves to the righteousness of God. This is a blunt statement of the fact, something Paul had already set forth in 2:17—3:8. The word *submit* means "to arrange under," "to put oneself under orders," "to obey."[5] This they refused to do. What

5. A. T. Robertson, *Word Pictures in the New Testament*, p. 387.

they were attempting to do was follow the external precepts of the law so they might demonstrate that they were personally righteous. On the basis of personal righteousness they were expecting to receive eternal life. By its very nature this excluded any thought or acceptance of a righteousness by faith. The righteousness of God by faith is the key to this chapter. This righteousness is within the reach of all, and it is intended for all, but not all of the Jews submitted themselves to it. This refusal to submit pointed to the very serious spiritual condition of these people. They were in point of fact insubordinate to God.

II. THE ACCESSIBILITY OF THE GOSPEL TO ALL (10:4-10)

The next few verses are intended to point out the fact that the gospel has been placed within the reach of all, that is to say, within the reach of all in the sense that its benefits, constituting a righteousness of God by faith, can become the experience and possession of any person. Paul unfolds this truth in this way:

A. **The expression of accessibility is set forth in verse 4.** Christ, a person, in His performance, is the end of the law. He brought the law to its end, or He put a stop to the law on the issues of righteousness by what He did at Calvary. There He took away the law which was "contrary to us" by "nailing it to his cross" (Col. 2:14). There He "abolished in his flesh the enmity, even the law of commandments contained in ordinances" (Eph. 2:15). There Christ satisfied the law's last holy demand for infraction, so that as a means of salvation it need never exercise any further control over any soul (Heb. 2:15). That person who has exercised faith in Christ for the righteousness which was made available at the cross is exhorted to "stand fast therefore in the liberty wherewith Christ hath made us free, and be not entangled again with the yoke of bondage" (Gal. 5:1).

B. **The exclusion of accessibility to life for every soul is accomplished by the law** (v. 5). Instead of righteousness being within the reach of all under the demands of the law, it works just the opposite. Moses declared in the Book of Leviticus (18:5) "that the man which doeth those things shall live by them. . . ." This meant that he was obligated to keep all of the law, all of the time, and each item must be kept perfectly. There was nothing wrong with this, except that no person had ever succeeded in meeting those qualifications. It was something the law could not do in that it was weak through the flesh (Rom. 8:3). In making this demand upon men, the law excluded men from righteousness instead of making it accessible to men. Recall the reference of Paul to his earlier life as "touching the righteousness which is in the law, blameless" (Phil. 3:6); he was blameless only before men and not God. And even the blamelessness before men was a mere external, mechanical blamelessness that was cold, heartless, and implacable.

C. The explanation of accessibility of the gospel is admirably set forth in the farewell address of Moses to the children of Israel in Deuteronomy 30:11-14 (vv. 6-8). In this account there are no impossible conditions laid down for the reception of righteousness. No spectacular feats are demanded of men. In fact no contribution is asked of anyone. No one is asked to ascend the heights of heaven and bring Christ down. And no one must make descent into the abyss to bring Christ up from the dead. No one need go anywhere to find the message of life. It is so near it is in the heart and mouth of everyone. All he needs to do is frame those words already in his possession into a simple statement of faith, and righteousness becomes his. The ministry of Christ from incarnation to resurrection is a work of God providing salvation to any trusting soul. Each Jewish person knew the facts about Christ, but he took those words and made them the subject of bitter controversy. All he needs to do now is take those same words and form them into a confession of faith, and he will be justified and granted life.

D. The exploitation of accessibility, that is, the utilization for profit, is accomplished by a confession of faith (vv. 9-10). This confession centers in the person of Christ. There must be genuine heart faith that Jesus is Lord and that this lordship was demonstrated by resurrection. This will be exhibited by confession of the mouth. Confession means to say with the mouth what agrees with the facts and corresponds with the conviction in the heart. Now Paul has struck at the real issue. It is the question concerning the identity of Christ. Is this Jesus of Nazareth none other than the promised Messiah, the Lord from heaven? Though Paul had once fought against this (I Tim. 1:13), at last he was forced to make confession of Christ as Lord (Acts 9:5). And he admitted later that no man can make this confession except by the Holy Spirit (I Cor. 12:3). But when the Holy Spirit of God reveals Christ in the heart (Gal. 1:16) and the man truly believes this great fact, he will then give voice to it by mouth. This will demonstrate the fact that he has experienced salvation.

III. THE OPPORTUNITY FOR ALL TO ACCEPT (10:11-15)

Paul's discussion would not be complete without clear reference to the fact that Israel has had opportunity to hear and respond to the gospel. The facts are that the gospel came to the Jews first (1:16). This means that the doctrine of divine election shuts no one out of the kingdom of God.

A. The universality of opportunity is therefore emphasized at the very outset (v. 11). This gospel is as wide in outreach as the entire human race. It is extended to "whosoever," and to complete its breadth of outreach the condition of faith is all that is necessary to experience its benefits. To support this argument to the Jew, the apostle combines two passages of Holy Writ (Isa. 28:16; 49:23). That person who grasps the right to believe and exercises the privilege to receive Christ will never be ashamed. He will never be confronted with any disappointment. He will find deliverance from the penalty of sin for righteousness; he will experience deliverance from the power and pollution of sin in holiness; he will shortly enter into deliverance from the presence of sin in glorification. Christ will not be a stone of stumbling to him nor the head of the corner in judgment, but a sanctuary of fellowship with the living God (Isa. 8:14; Ps. 118:22).

B. The impartiality of opportunity is therefore guaranteed to all (v. 12). "Just as there was no difference between Jew and Gentile with respect to sin and condemnation, so also there is no difference between them with respect to the offer of righteousness and salvation"[6] (see Rom. 3:22-23). Even though the gospel came to the Jew first, this was only a priority in time, because in the plan of God it was through the Jews that He intended to reach the Gentiles. Being the God of Jews and Gentiles alike, God put no difference between them in making the riches of His grace available to both. The poet Cowper caught the blessedness of this great truth.

> O! how unlike the complex works of man,
> Heaven's easy artless, unencumber'd plan!
> No meretricious graces to beguile,
> No clustering ornaments to clog the pile;
> From ostentation as from weakness free,
> It stands like the cerulean arch we see,
> Majestic in its own simplicity.
> Inscrib'd above the portal, from afar,
> Conspicuous as the brightness of a star,
> Legible only by the light they give,
> Stand the soul-quick'ning words—"Believe and live!"[7]

C. The realization of opportunity waits upon the heartfelt call of the sinner (v. 13). To carry the significance of opportunity and personal responsibility to the heart of the Jews, the apostle cites a passage from Joel to support this point (2:32). Out of a context that deals with the closing days of the age when judgment threatens mankind, and from which there is no possible human escape, the apostle extracts a principle and applies it to the Jew in his desperate situation. Just as a frantic soul can find deliverance from physical calamity by calling on the Lord, so he can

6. McClain, *The Jewish Problem and Its Divine Solution,* p. 19.
7. W. H. Griffith Thomas, *The Devotional Commentary: Romans Vol. II,* p. 173 (Cowper, Truth - quoted).

experience deliverance from spiritual calamity by calling on the Lord. The exercise of personal responsibility by calling on the Lord will place him in that remnant which the Lord will save. "Thus the door is opened just as wide as the word 'whosoever' can open it. No man can ever say that he was shut out from the divine provision of righteousness at Calvary. Yet those who lay hold on this righteousness are always those called and chosen."[8]

D. The implementation of opportunity constitutes the groundwork for missionary activity (vv. 14-15). The call of a sinner on the Lord requires that he believe. Believing must have an object and a compendium of truth above that object. So a message must come within the hearing of the sinner. If a message is to reach the sinner, then there must be a mouthpiece to herald that message. And if there is to be a herald of the truth, there must be a divine commission resting upon an individual. A quotation from Isaiah relating to the mediatorial kingdom and the place of Jews in heralding the gospel message to Gentiles clinches the point (Isa. 52:7). A vast number of men have not heard the gospel, as Paul well knows. Upon the believers at Rome he now uses this occasion to press home the responsibility for seeing that the gospel reaches the unevangelized. It is God's will that men be saved. Salvation depends upon the exercise of human responsibility toward the message of life. But there is a means to an end; it is the effort expended by saved people to see that the gospel reaches lost men. This means that divine sovereignty does not render human effort unnecessary. If sinners are to be held responsible for their sin and guilt, then the church will be held responsible for reaching sinners with the gospel of saving grace.

IV. THE INFLEXIBILITY OF JEWS TOWARD THE GOSPEL (10:16-21)

Though Paul used the occasion to press home a truth to saved people in the church at Rome, he is primarily dealing with Jews

8. McClain, *The Jewish Problem and Its Divine Solution*, p. 19.

who have heard the gospel and have refused to respond in faith. So in verse 16 he returns to the mainstream of his discourse and pursues it to its conclusion. So far Jewry in general has displayed a strong inflexibility to every approach of the gospel. This was true in Paul's day, and it remains true to this hour. Now Paul will touch on the evidence (vv. 16-17), the universality (v. 18), the occasion (vv. 19-20), and the tragedy (v. 21).

A. The evidence of inflexibility is the refusal to obey the message of the gospel (vv. 16-17). It is a startling fact that they have not all obeyed the gospel. To enlarge upon that fact it must be pointed out that most of the Jews had rejected the message. Those who had responded constituted a small flock (Luke 12:32). The rank and file had turned their backs on the Christian faith, and that is the reason that as a nation Israel was unsaved.

But the fault is not to be charged against God. The proof for this is a Scripture cited from Isaiah. The prophet, foreseeing the present unbelief of his people, introduces that precious chapter of his prophecies with the words, "Who hath believed our report?" (53:1). This report was of a suffering servant of the Lord:

> For he shall grow up before him as a tender plant, and as a root out of dry ground: he hath no form nor comeliness; and when we shall see him, there is no beauty that we should desire him. He is despised and rejected of men; a man of sorrows, and acquainted with grief: and we hid as it were our faces from him; he was despised, and we esteemed him not. Surely he hath borne our griefs, and carried our sorrows: yet we did esteem him stricken, smitten of God, and afflicted. But he was wounded for our transgressions, he was bruised for our iniquities: the chastisement of our peace was upon him; and with his stripes we are healed. All we like sheep have gone astray; we have turned every one to his own way; and the Lord hath laid on him the iniquity of us all (Isa. 53:2-6).

Just as hearing is essential to faith in order for the discharge of human responsibility, hearing the message and rejecting it is also a discharge of responsibility for which there is accountability.

B. The universality of inflexibility is described in language taken from Psalm 19 (v. 18). Some Jews might complain that they did not have an opportunity to hear the message, but Paul denies this. They did have an opportunity to hear. The organization of Jewry made it possible for them to hear. The temple was yet standing, and even though the Jews were scattered far and wide across the world, they were obliged to have representatives at the feast in Jerusalem. Sometimes as many as several million Jews made pilgrimage to the Holy City. Two great feasts were just fifty days apart: the Passover and Pentecost. At the Passover these Jews witnessed the crucifixion of Christ. At Pentecost they heard the message of Christ's death and resurrection. Thousands were saved and went back to their homes with the message about Christ (Acts 2:5 ff.). This explains why Christians were spoken against everywhere (Acts 28:22). Those Jews who heard, therefore, could not plead ignorance on the one hand or lack of understanding on the other. It is therefore a fair statement to say that their rigid stand against the gospel was universal.

C. The occasion for inflexibility was in part to be traced to the fact that the Gentiles did respond to the gospel (vv. 19-20). However, some in Israel—perhaps many—took refuge in the excuse that they did not know. But that could hardly stand in court when Gentiles who were completely outside the pale of knowledge concerning Scriptural things responded to the gospel. Moses foretold the fact that God would provoke the Jews to jealousy and anger by Gentile acceptance of the gospel (Deut. 32:21). Paul well remembered the occasions when he made reference to Gentiles, inciting the wrath of the Jews to the point that he was forced to flee (Acts 13:46-50; 22:21-24). Isaiah spoke even more plainly on this point. He predicted that men who were in no sense seeking for the Lord, when confronted with the gospel, would believe it (Isa. 65:1). This can only mean that the gospel message is so simple as set forth beforehand in the Jewish prophets that Gentiles could apprehend the message and were encouraged to accept it.

D. The tragedy of inflexibility on the part of the Jew centered in his own heart (v. 21). The gospel message was not something that was far off, inaccessible, designed for the few, and hard to be understood. The whole trouble was to be traced to hearts confirmed in unbelief. In this state there was a determination of the will to reject. No amount of evidence made any impact on them. In fact they were not seeking evidence. What they wanted was their own way. And that way was to exalt themselves by pursuing the righteousness of the law. Long ago the prophet Isaiah described the hopelessness of the situation. Speaking of the Lord, the prophet pictured the prolonged effort to reach the people. All day long he stretched forth his hands in pleading to no avail. They were not only disobedient to the call for salvation, but they indulged themselves in talking back to the Lord and justifying their refusal. In this note of tragedy the chapter ends. Israel has been given every opportunity to come to the Lord and has rejected. Therefore God is vindicated with respect to the righteousness of His dealings with Israel. Unsaved Jews have no one to blame for their lost condition but themselves.

Questions for Individual Study

1. What is the theme of chapter 10? Does it in any sense retreat from the teaching in chapter 9?
2. Where does Paul place the blame for the unsaved condition of the Jew? Be specific.
3. In what sense was Christ the end of the law for righteousness?
4. Explain how the law excluded men from salvation.
5. Did the Jews have opportunity to accept the gospel? How wide was the offer?
6. Is there anything about human responsibility that lays the groundwork for missionary activity?
7. Why is the Jew wrong in claiming that he had not heard, or did not know about the gospel?

Chapter 9

The Merciful Purpose of God in Israel

Romans 11:1-36

The concluding and crowning chapter in the argument of the apostle concerning Israel now comes into view. In some sense this chapter is central to the whole epistle. Without the background of the preceding chapters it would be impossible to reach this point. But if it were possible to start at this point with comprehension, the preceding chapters would be more easily understood.

The ascription of praise with which this chapter concludes (vv. 33-36) is the pinnacle finally reached in the progressive unfolding of this gigantic theme. If it were possible to begin here it would be possible to look down on the movements of God's providence among men and see the amazing and intricate developments through the eyes of God. Fragmented thought and limited perspective would be swallowed up in the fulness of vision of the program of God. Every segment of truth would then be completely articulated and integrated in the whole plan of God.

It would then be possible to see that there is one eternal purpose running through the entire course of history. And that purpose is the dominant theme of the entire Book of Romans as well as of chapters 9 through 11. At its center is mercy toward all mankind, as well as to Israel; and its end result is to contribute to the glory of God (11:32, 36). Chapter 11 of the epistle brings this purpose into full focus in relation to the nation of Israel. While it is true that history sheds light on the Bible, there is nothing more significant than that the Bible, and especially this chapter, sheds light on history. Israel, an enigma among nations, is the focal point of God's purpose in history.

Dispensational truth is brought into clear relief at this point. It was Augustine who said, "Distinguish the dispensations, and the Scriptures will agree." His observation could not be more appropriate than in the chapter at hand. It is impossible to understand God's design for the nation of Israel apart from the recognition of the fact that the administration of God varies with different companies of people and in different periods of time. When once this becomes clear, it will be seen that through all the varying administrations there runs one eternal purpose. Israel, the nations, and the church do not lose their identity or distinctiveness, but each performs its function in contributing to that one eternal purpose.

In this chapter Israel is under consideration as a nation rather than as individuals. After all that has been said in the preceding chapters, the question is—What is the present status of Israel as a nation?

> The covenant with Abraham is here referred to his natural seed and is regarded as a permanent validity. It is inaccurate to speak of the Jews as God's "ancient" people. They are His "permanent" people, because of the perpetuity of the Divine covenant with Abraham. We must beware of spiritualizing the Old Testament and making references to Israel and Jacob refer to the Church. Much of the Old Testament remains unfulfilled to this day . . . . The preservation of the Jews today is a proof of this perpetual covenant of God with Israel.[1]

According to Paul there is no canceling of the ancient promises and privileges granted to Israel. "For the gifts and calling of God are without repentance" (11:29). On this firm foundation the apostle discusses the present status of Israel, not as a "spiritual Israel" but as a national entity that traces its lineage back to Abraham. The final verse of chapter 10 and the opening verse of chapter 11 establish this connection. Any other approach to this subject makes the issue at hand vanish in a mist of subjectivism. In the literal nation of Israel, the eternal purpose of God is now brought into bold relief.

1. W. H. Griffith Thomas, The Devotional Commentary: Romans Vol. II, pp. 224-25.

I. THE CONFRONTATION WITH THE PURPOSE OF GOD IN ISRAEL (11:1)

A. The presentation of the problem at hand is brought into clear view by a question: "Hath God cast away his people?" It is even more vivid in the Greek, for the form of the question expects a negative answer. Could the matter be more vividly confronted than to state the question this way? He has just made reference to "a disobedient and gainsaying people" (10:21) as set forth in the prophecy of Isaiah (65:2). And Isaiah was contrasting this nation with Gentile nations (65:1). As a whole this people had turned from the truth of God to idolatry and were spurning every appeal of the Lord to return to Him. This was true in Isaiah's day, and it continued unvaryingly. It was true in the day of Christ when this nation rejected its King, the Lord Jesus Christ. And it was true as Paul sought to reach his people. Now, has God cast away this nation of people?

B. The opposition to the thought of being cast away is vigorously stated: "God forbid." Let it not be. Knowing the truth on this point, the apostle states the fact and later points to the proof. The proof may not be so easily comprehended, but the emphatic denial cannot be missed by anyone. But the denial does prepare the reader for the proof that is to come. It alerts him to what he should expect to find in the succeeding words of the apostle. And this in turn will help him to find a way of interpreting what the apostle is saying.

C. The argumentation of the point begins with a personal reference to himself: "For I also am an Israelite, of the seed of Abraham, of the tribe of Benjamin." The word "for" is a particle introducing logical argument. As proof he cites himself. He is of the seed of Abraham according to the flesh and belongs to the tribe of Benjamin. He is convinced that he has not been cast away, and this is preeminently true because the grace of God has reached him. By the same token the grace of God will reach the nation as a nation. Therefore it is true that God has not cast away His people.

II. THE CORROBORATION OF THE PURPOSE OF GOD IN ISRAEL (11:2-12)

To his emphatic denial the apostle adds a declarative statement: "God hath not cast away his people which he foreknew. . . ." (v. 2a). This is probably an echo of the Old Testament scripture which he knows so well (I Sam. 12:22; Ps. 94:14). "The whole course of Israel's history was thus foreseen and foreknown, and at no point did God ever contemplate ceasing to be their faithful covenant-keeping God."[2] This nation is His people. In spite of what He knew about them, what would develop in the course of the centuries, He chose them. And this suggests that foreknowledge carries with it the impartation of grace to make them in fact what they are in name. In order to establish this point the writer marshals collective proof.

A. He first points to a perpetual remnant in the original divine purpose for Israel (vv. 2-6). His argument really began in reference to himself as an Israelite, of the seed of Abraham, of the tribe of Benjamin. Then he moves to Scripture, describing the situation in Israel during the days of Elijah (I Kings 19:9-18). Those were dark days. Apostasy had run its course through the rank and file of the Northern Kingdom. An evil queen, Jezebel, was serving as the priestess of Baal, and Elijah himself was the object of her anger. As far as Elijah could see there were none to take their stand with him, and the cause of God in Israel was lost. In that dark hour a still, small voice whispered encouragement to him and informed him that there were seven thousand who had not bowed the knee to Baal nor kissed the image (I Kings 19:2-18). Just as in that day God reserved to Himself a remnant, "even so then at this present time also there is a remnant according to the election of grace." Since this is an election of grace and not of works, then it is of faith, and the purpose of God is fulfilled in the creation of a peculiar people according to the flesh who believe on the Lord Jesus Christ.[3]

2. Thomas, p. 191.
3. G. Campbell Morgan, The Analyzed Bible: Romans, pp. 172-73.

B. There is a partial fulfillment of the divine purpose in the Gentiles (vv. 7-11). The expression "What then?" suggests that the complete story has not yet been told. The nation of Israel did not obtain what it sought for, a righteousness by means of law (9:31); but the election obtained a righteousness by faith (Deut. 7:6), whereas all the rest in Israel were hardened (ASV). An insensitivity fell upon them that was complete. They slumbered in the face of approaching peril; their eyes could not penetrate through the mist of doubt; their ears became dull toward the warning of the prophets (Isa. 29:10). David grasped the situation and committed them to the snare, the trap, to stumbling, to a recompense they deserved for they crucified their Messiah (Ps. 69:20-23; 28:4). Their stumbling, however, was not a stumbling merely to fall and nothing more. Paul vigorously denies this. But their fall, and here the word means "to fall aside" or "make a misstep," leads to something wonderful. It brought salvation to the Gentiles (Isa. 42:6-7; Acts 28:24, 28), and in turn this provoked the Jews (Deut. 32:21). But by this means God was able to bring to realization a portion of His promise to Abraham (Gen. 12:3) in which Gentiles become the spiritual seed of Abraham (Gal. 3:7-9, 29).

C. There is yet a perfect fulfillment in the purpose of God for Israel (v. 12). Though Paul now introduces a question, it is merely a rhetorical device, the answer to which is obvious. Since the fall of Israel set them aside for a time and resulted in God turning to the larger world of mankind with the riches of His grace, and since the diminution of Israel for the moment issued in granting to the Gentiles a plentitude which they had never known, is it not logical that the fulness of Israel will unfold in benefits to the Gentiles far beyond anything ever dreamed? The answer Paul expects and knows will be true is an affirmative. When this finally takes place, then all that God intended for Israel will be realized (Deut. 7:6; Exod. 19:5-6; Gen. 12:3); then all the claims Israel made for herself will blossom into reality (Rom. 2:17-20); then there will be a perfect fulfillment of the divine purpose in Israel (Ps. 72:8-11; Isa. 60:3; 61:6; 62:1-4).

Today God is working among Gentiles to take out of them a people for His name. But in due time this work will come to completion and the Lord will call the church out of this world. He will then turn again to His people Israel and will bring them to Himself, that in turn He may work through them and reach all the Gentile nations (Acts 15:14-17). This will be the greatest day in the history of mankind. It will mark the greatest period of evangelization in the history of the world.

III. THE CONFORMATION TO THE PURPOSE OF GOD IN ISRAEL (11:13-24)

Carrying the theme of the preceding verses a step further, the writer now shows how Israel will conform to the purpose God intended for this nation. An abundance of fruit in Israel is yet future and will produce an amazing response among Gentiles (vv. 13-16). However, the present attitude in Israel is no reason for rejoicing on the part of Gentiles. They too will be held accountable (vv. 17-31). The proper approach in both cases is to evaluate the activity of God (vv. 22-24).

A. **Abundant fruitfulness is God's purpose for Israel in the future** (vv. 13-16). But the apostle is not satisfied to wait for the future to see fruit in his people. So he addresses the Gentiles with a message to arouse in them such activity as will produce immediate response among his own people. He would like to see some of them saved now. He is perfectly within his right to appeal to the Gentile Christians because he is the apostle to the Gentiles, and he ought to make the most out of his office.

It is a fact that the temporary casting away of Israel worked in such a way that it brought about the reconciling of the world. God permitted the Jews to go their way. In hardness of heart and blindness of spirit they did not recognize or receive their own Messiah, but instead rebelled against Him and rejected Him. This led to the tragedy of Calvary, as seen from one vantage point; but on the other hand it was a victory. God turned it into a triumph for all mankind (Acts 2:23; I Peter 1:18-20; II Cor. 5:19).

Since temporary rejection led to reconciliation, surely the permanent reception of Israel can only lead to resurrection. Some think that is the sense of this statement. But on the other hand it may be figurative at this point, in which case he is saying that salvation of the Jews will produce such an amazing response from among Gentiles that there will be world revival. Jews will become the messengers of God's grace to the world of Gentiles, and in the tribulation and millennium millions will be swept into the kingdom of God (Acts 15:14-17).

It is a fact that the firstfruit was holy, the patriarchs of old, Abraham, Isaac, Jacob; therefore the lump, the abundance of the harvest, must also be holy even though it is yet future. The root of Israel was Abraham. He was holy, so what comes from him, the branches, must also be holy. In the firstfruit and the root there is the promise of the branches and the harvest. "The spiritual glories of the patriarchs are thus regarded as the earnest of the future which awaits the race."[4]

B. Gentile accountability must never be forgotten (vv. 17-21). At this point it is important that the horticultural figure be carefully considered, so that false conclusions may be avoided.

> Some interpreters, taking this tree in verses 16-24 as representing either Christ or the Church, find here some support for the unscriptural theory that a true Christian may lose his place in Christ. A little horticultural knowledge should be sufficient to refute such an interpretation. As every competent horticulturist knows, the grafting of a wild olive branch among the natural branches does not change the nature of the wild olive in any degree. In other words, in Paul's olive tree Jews remain Jews, and Gentiles remain Gentiles. But in Christ there is neither Jew nor Gentile; all such distinctions cease. It is best therefore to regard the olive tree as representing the place of favor or privilege before God. Abraham is the root, for through him and his seed the favor of God has flowed into the world. The natural branches are Jewish, because "Salvation is of the Jews." But on account of unbelief certain of the natural branches were broken out, and wild Gentile branches were grafted in. This does not mean that all the Gentile branches are

4. Thomas, *The Devotional Commentary: Romans Vol. II,* p. 200.

saved any more than that all the former Jewish branches were saved. As a matter of fact, they were not saved, or they would not have been broken out. But it does mean that during the present age the Gentile is enjoying a place of favor which properly belongs to the Jew. The chief point of the illustration is this: If God spared not the natural branches when they failed to live up to the responsibility of their favored position, neither will He spare the wild branches if they fail to take advantage of the favor shown them. Therefore, it does not behoove the Gentiles to be "high-minded" or to glory over the natural branches, for God is fully able to graft the Jew back into the tree of favor. After all, this place belongs properly to the Jew. The tree is "their own."[5]

C. It is the activity of God in the working out of His purpose that deserves attention (vv. 22-24). Take a look at the goodness and severity of God. It was unbelief that brought the infliction of severity on Israel. It was goodness that placed the Gentiles in the place of favor. And that goodness will continue to be manifest so long as Gentiles continue in that goodness. Continuation requires the exercise of faith. When the nation of Israel forsakes its unbelief for faith, it will again be inducted into the place of favor. Since the Gentiles by grace were inducted into the place of favor, they may be sure that God will more than restore Israel in that place to fulfill His original purpose for Israel. In this passage we see divine sovereignty and human responsibility working together.

IV. THE CALCULATION OF THE PURPOSE OF GOD IN ISRAEL (11:25-32)

As the apostle draws the argument to a conclusion he makes some final calculation on various aspects of the purpose of God in Israel. He points to the great mystery of Israel's blindness (v. 25). A stupendous miracle will be enacted in the restoration of Israel (vv. 26-27). But the overall character and purpose of God will be exhibited in His tender mercy toward all (vv. 28-32).

---

5. Alva J. McClain, *The Jewish Problem and Its Divine Solution*, pp. 25-26.

A. **The mystery of Israel's blindness is a matter of which Gentile believers ought not to be ignorant** (v. 25). Ignorance at this point can lead to a sophistication that grows out of pure conceit. By this he means that you can draw false conclusions because you do not see in perspective all the facts relating to the blindness. As has been demonstrated down across the Christian era, it has led Gentiles to believe that they were somehow better than Jews. Did not the Jews crucify Christ? But this is utterly false. Christ died because of the sin of all people. And representatively Gentiles as well as Jews were implicated in the crucifixion. Note, however, that the blindness in Israel is incomplete and temporary. Some Jews have come to Christ down through the Christian centuries, even though the vast majority have rejected Him. But this blindness of the many will last only till the fulness of the Gentiles is come in. "Fulness" must have reference to the present age of the church during which God is taking out from among the Gentiles a people for His name (Acts 15:14). When the last soul of those chosen from among the Gentiles answers the call of the gospel, the fulness will be complete. Then God will turn again to Israel and place the nation in the very center of His operations. But until then Israel is dispersed from the land and suffers persecution (Luke 21:24).

B. **The miracle of Israel's salvation takes place following the fulness of the Gentiles** (vv. 26-27). All Israel will be saved. This can only mean that the blindness is lifted. Out of Zion will come the great Deliverer, the Lord Jesus Christ. They will recognize Him and call upon Him and call Him blessed (Matt. 23:39). And the Lord will turn away ungodliness from Jacob. Moreover, God will fulfill His covenant with the nation of Israel in turning them away from sin (Isa. 27:9; Jer. 31:31-37). Not only will they recognize the Messiah and confess their sin (Isa. 53:1-6), but God will write His laws on their hearts and in their minds. All this is associated with the second coming of Christ. At His coming in power and glory, Israel will recognize in this victorious Sovereign the Man of sorrows who died for their sins. "And one shall say unto him, What are these wounds in thine hands? Then he shall answer, Those with which I was wounded in the house of my friends" (Zech. 13:6). And God "will pour upon the house of David, and upon the inhabitants of Jerusalem, the spirit of grace and of supplications: and they shall look upon me whom they have pierced, and they shall mourn for him, as one mourneth for his only son, and shall be in bitterness for him, as one that is in bitterness for his firstborn" (Zech. 12:10). And a nation shall be born at once (Isa. 66:8).

C. The mercy of God toward all mankind is central in the outworking of God's purpose for Israel (vv. 28-32). From the standpoint of the gospel Israel is the enemy of God for the sake of Gentiles. That is, God used this defection of Israel as an occasion to turn to the Gentiles. But from the standpoint of God's choice of Israel, Israel is beloved for the sake of the fathers upon whom He moved in favor at the beginning. This means the gifts and calling of God are without repentance. God never changes His mind, and He may be trusted to carry His purpose through to its culmination. In time past Gentiles did not believe in God, but now they have experienced the mercy of God because Jews were unbelieving. But unbelieving Jews will yet enter into the mercy of God because God has shown mercy to Gentiles. This may all be concluded in one point that God has shut up all men in one prison house of disobedience that He might have mercy on all. This is a remarkable demonstration of how God forces sin to serve the purpose of His mercy.[6]

V. THE CONCLUSION OF THE PURPOSE OF GOD IN ISRAEL (11:33-36)

The doxology with which chapter 11 comes to a close is really a rapturous burst of praise covering the entire system of theology in the Book of Romans—and, for that matter, the Bible.

A. The inexhaustibleness of God is the initial emphasis of the doxology (v. 33). There is a depth of riches, and wisdom, and

6. Thomas, *The Devotional Commentary: Romans Vol. II,* p. 213.

knowledge that is unfathomable. The wealth of His grace is superabundant; the wisdom of His ways in immediate acts and providential arrangements is multiple; the knowledge of God is omniscient, covering the past, the present, and the future. These cannot be searched out or tracked down.

B. The independence of God sets Him aside in splendor and loneliness (vv. 34-35). God is completely isolated from all others. No one knows His mind, and He is indebted to no one for counsel (Isa. 40:13). Everything is possessed by Him so He is not the object of any gratuity from anyone. This means that He is not obligated to any, for He is the source of everything (I Chron. 29:11-14).

C. The initiative always rests with God in everything and this is so in salvation (v. 36a). He is the source from which things come. He is the channel by which they are ministered to men. He is the destination toward which they move. Salvation proceeds from God. He is the One who channels it to men. He is the final destination and purpose toward which salvation moves. Anything short of this is not the salvation of God. And evermore He is acting under the constraint of all-conquering power and all-consuming love.

D. The inscription to God is one of glory (v. 36b). It has been said that no one has really learned the meaning of this epistle until he can join with Paul in this ascription of praise: "to him be glory for ever. Amen." This is a recognition of what God is: inscrutable wisdom, invincible might, interminable grace, inextinguishable love. Glory is the sum total of all the attributes of God: His greatness, His goodness, His glory. When the plan of God is completely fulfilled in men, all created intelligences will acknowledge His glory forever. This is so true that Paul seals it with the word "Amen." Let it be so absolutely. This word guarantees its fulfillment, for it is the name of Christ (Rev. 3:14). Now that the veil of mystery has been torn aside, the heart comes to rest in Him where all fulness dwells (Col. 1:19).

Questions for Individual Study

1. What place does chapter 11 have in relation to the preceding chapters of Romans?
2. Is the apostle discussing the future of Israel as a nation or as individuals?
3. How does Paul introduce the subject of the chapter, and what is his immediate response?
4. What threefold argument does Paul cite to prove that God has not cast away Israel?
5. How did God use the temporary defection of Israel as an occasion for blessing to Gentiles?
6. How does Paul use the olive tree, the natural branches, and the wild branches to illustrate a truth?
7. How is the mystery of Israel's blindness a matter Gentiles need to understand?

Chapter 10

Transformation in the Personal Conduct of Believers
Romans 12:1-21

In the hush and esctasy of prostration before an ineffable God, as the great doctrinal section of the Book of Romans comes to its close, transition is made to the practical section in which the eternal truths are applied to Christian life. The word "therefore" links all that is about to be said with all that has already been said. The succeeding chapters of the epistle constitute exposition of what precedes and enforcement in life. In these chapters we shall see how the forces of grace issue in fruition in the lives of saints.

In the first eleven chapters of this epistle the writer has presented the all-encompassing theological system covering the subject of salvation. In this division he argued convincingly for the infliction of wrath upon sinful mankind (1:18—3:20). He set forth the method of providing a righteousness of God for salvation (3:21—8:39). And he demonstrated clearly the wisdom of God in His methods of reaching Jews and Gentiles (9:1—11:36). Now that the theological foundation has been firmly laid and it has been demonstrated that the methods of God with men are sovereign, supreme, sufficient and sublime in ministering blessing to the entire human race, Paul turns to God's claims upon saved men.

In the chapters before us, there is one guiding principle: the will of God. The key to this section hangs at the door. It is that believers shall be transformed that they may prove the will of God (12:2). This provides the answer for the question how saved men should live. There should be progressive transformation from within produced by the renewing of the mind. It is the person of Christ as reflected in the Word of God that displays in graphic form what God's will is for each saint. Commensurate with the apprehension of Christ as set forth in the Word of God, there will be progressive transformation into the likeness of Christ (II Cor. 3:18).

The importance of the order in the transmission of truth in the Epistle to the Romans is of high importance. Until the saints recognize what they are saved *from* as well as what they are saved *to*, in addition to the salvation that provides sufficiency to save them, it is impossible to encourage them to appropriate these benefits by the exercise of human responsibility. So the apostle followed the usual pattern in his epistles by presenting principles, then turning to practice; first doctrine, then duty; first revelation, then responsibility. He is now ready to confront believers with the meaning of responsibility in various areas of life.[1]

As the apostle well knows, it is at this point where Christian responsibility encounters personal opposition. The old nature still dwells within and resists subordination to holiness. It is therefore absolutely necessary to keep Christian doctrine in the forefront of the consciousness. This is accomplished only by the renewing of the mind. It is in this way that the believer makes constant appropriation of the benefits of Christ and is therefore enabled to move toward that blessed goal of being conformed to the image of Christ (Rom. 8:29). What has gone before in this epistle therefore provides the dynamics for the enactment to follow. With impassioned appeal the apostle urges believers to move forward to the discovery of God's will for their lives.

The final division of the epistle consists of five chapters covering in general the various areas of Christian responsibility. In chapter 12 believers are urged to apply the will of God to their own individual lives. Chapter 13 is designed to guide believers into the will of God in relation to political alignments. Chapter 14 covers the will of God as it relates to Christian fellowship.

---

1. Alva J. McClain, *The Epistle to the Romans Outlined and Summarized*, p. 38.

And chapters 15-16 point out how the will of God should characterize personal contribution to the Christian community and the
world.

At this point we turn to chapter 12. In this chapter appear
three different aspects of Christian responsibility: the presentation of self to God (vv. 1-2); the humiliation of self for service
(vv. 3-8); and the dedication of self to others (vv. 9-21).

I. THE PRESENTATION OF SELF TO GOD (12:1-2)

There is a sense in which verses 1 and 2 constitute the primary
and central appeal of the entire book. It is directed to special
people (v. 1a), possesses a providential basis (v. 1b), calls for
personal presentation (v. 1c), displayed by progressive transformation (v. 2a), and proving the perfect will of God (v. 2b).

**A. Christian people are the objects of this practical appeal for
presentation** (v. 1a). They are called "brethren." This means that
the apostle assumes that on the basis of a genuine profession of
faith in Christ they have experienced the miracle of regenera-
tion. They have been born into the family of God. Since the word
brethren signifies those who have come forth from the same
womb, he is implying that they have been born again by the
Spirit of God. They now share in the vital blessings of the new
nature and are kin to one another and to Paul. This means that
they also have a new relationship with God. He is now their
Father and they are responsible to be subject to Him as children.
Within this new family there are mutual relationships and obligations, and one of those is to exhort one another (Heb. 10:25).
The new position which these people now enjoy does not relieve
them of obligation. In fact this new position in Christ imposes
obligation for living like members of the family of God. This
explains the presence of the word "therefore."

B. The providential basis for this appeal is the mercies of God
(v. 1b). This appeal derives its force "by" or "through" these
mercies. The first eleven chapters of the book provide the saint
with adequate unfolding of the character of these mercies of

God. There is nothing in that whole section that describes what man is to do for God that can be called mercies. To the contrary, that whole section is devoted to what God has done for man in justification, sanctification, preservation, and integration. These mercies are the channel through which man has been brought into the family of God and to the place of service. Viewing these mercies from the position of prostration one sees the wonders of God's grace which provides the occasion and the incentive for responding to any appeal from God. Beyond the pale of these mercies one might ask why he should do anything for God. After all, what has He done for me? The answer is clear. Take a look at the mercies of God.

C. A personal presentation of self is urged for every saint (v. 1c). "Present your bodies a living sacrifice. . . ." The tense of the verb "present," an aorist, suggests taking decisive action, that of standing alongside or delivering to God the body. This is not to be confused with conversion, although it could take place at the same time as conversion. In most cases it is something that will take place some time subsequent to conversion, usually at that time when full comprehension of the mercies of God elicits the obligation they entail. The word "present" is the same word used in Romans 6:13, 19 and translated "yield." It was that which the priest performed in offering Levitical sacrifices (Lev. 1:3; 16:7). It was what the parents of Christ did when they came to the temple with Christ "to present him to the Lord" (Luke 2:22). This is an action that should be done once for all in the lifetime, although there may be need for renewal of its significance from time to time.

This is a handing over of the body to God, not as a mere carcass of flesh and blood and bone, but as *an organism* consisting of spirit and soul and body—that is, the whole man. This includes all that he is in the course of all time. Unlike Old Testament sacrifices, this is to be "a living sacrifice," that is, a sacrifice capable of doing something. It is not a giving of something to God which we would rather not part with. To the contrary it is a delight to hand oneself over to Him. Dead sacrifices are a thing of the past. Now the Lord wants living sacrifices. One could die in a moment of time. But this calls for more. As living, all that he is and does for all time is now being presented to the Lord. And what the Lord calls for is something that is holy and acceptable to God. As holy, it is something that is not only set apart to God in position, but also in practice. This means something clean in spirit, soul, and body. As acceptable, it is something that is well pleasing to God, delighting His heart because it represents praise and gratitude for His benefits (14:18; II Cor. 5:9; Eph. 5:10; Phil. 4:18; Heb. 13:16, 21).[2]

This presentation of the body is something that is *reasonable*. Though the American Standard Version has chosen to render this word "spiritual" it hardly gets at the basic meaning. More literally rendered it is the word *logical*. It means that certain things which in point of fact have been experienced by the believer call for a response which grows out of reason. The mercies of God actually served the purpose of purchasing the believers. They have been bought with a price (I Cor. 6:19-20). This means they are not their own; they belong to the One who purchased them. It is therefore altogether reasonable for the Owner to ask them to hand themselves over to Him. In its highest performance this act of presentation will indeed be spiritual, but in basic significance it is reasonable. Levitical priests offered sacrifices totally unlike and separate from themselves, but Christian believers have nothing else to offer but themselves. Nothing could be more acceptable to God, for the believer is something like God in image by creation (Gen. 1:26-27), and is something exactly like God by new creation (Eph. 5:24).

D. Progressive transformation of the self is a further aspect of the appeal (v. 2a). A twofold response is associated with this appeal. On the one hand the believer is urged to "be not conformed to this world." To put this in other terms, he is to stop masquerading in the forms of this age. The root of the word "conformed" means a form appearing on the outside but obscur-

2. J. Agar Beet, *St. Paul's Epistle to the Romans*, p. 316.

ing the nature on the inside. Since they now have a new nature, believers should not be conducting themselves in such a way that they conceal the new nature. They should stop the sort of life style that marked their preconversion days. After all, habits, styles, mannerisms, speech, enjoyments, and employment belong to this present age, and therefore as temporary and passing should come to an end.

In the place of a process of masquerading, there should be a *progressive transformation* into the likeness of Christ. Here the word "transformed" has a root which points to a form on the outside that clearly reveals the nature on the inside. From this word is derived the English word *metamorphosis*. This word is used to describe the change that takes place from caterpillar stage to butterfly. In the fall of the year the caterpillar builds a cocoon in which during the long winter months it undergoes metamorphosis. When it breaks forth from the cocoon in the spring it possesses all the intricate framework and delicate hues of the butterfly. A person seeing it in this form calls it a butterfly, which in fact it is, as indicated by its external form. This change proceeds from the inside to the outside and is progressive, moving from one stage to another. This is the pathway to spiritual maturity.

In the case of the believer this is accomplished by *the renewing of the mind*. The substance for renewing the mind is the Word of God, which consists of the will of God. Therein is the perfect image of the Son of God and the details of life which are pleasing to the Lord. As these things gradually condition the mind of the saint, the impulse to walk in this way issues in the conduct of the believer. The compulsion proceeds entirely from within and there is no feeling of external control. There is no feeling of bondage, for freedom is after all the set of the will in relation to reality. As the believer grows in knowledge he also grows in grace. And as grace molds his will there is consequent and commensurate development into the likeness of Christ. "But whoso keepeth his word, in him verily is the love of God perfected: hereby know we that we are in him. He that saith he abideth in him ought himself also so to walk, even as he walked" (I John 2:5-6). This emphasizes the importance of Bible study. It pinpoints the value of daily devotions. It makes clear that growth in grace is vitally associated with intimate involvement with the Word of God.

E. The ultimate destination of this process is the final discovery of the will of God for the individual life. This is expressed in the text by the words "that ye may prove what is that good, and acceptable, and perfect, will of God." Surely no sincere soul among the saints desires anything more precious than this. To find this is to find that place of rest and satisfaction that nothing else can supply. There is nothing so disturbing or distressing as to grope through the darkness of this world, never sure that one is traveling the right road. To be sure that one is on the right road gives that courage of conviction that enables one to face the hardships, the heartaches, and the hazards of life in full assurance that there will eventually be a day of triumph and crowning; that there will be a day of manifestation when it will be made perfectly clear that the Christian life was worth living; that the way one walked was good, and acceptable, and perfect in fulfilling the plan of God.

This proving or testing of the will of God is progressive. It does not take place all at once, as indicated by the present tense of the verb. It parallels the renewing of the mind. The constant involvement with the Word of God enables the believer to evaluate the areas of conduct and select that which the Word of God approves. Every step in the direction of that perfect will brings with it the accompanying inward satisfaction that he is on the right road and moving in the direction for the final triumph. To do that which is good is to be like God. To do that which is acceptable is to be well pleasing to God. To do that which is perfect is to lack nothing that is necessary for the full approval of the Lord. In all this there is the progressive display of the excellencies of Him who called us out of darkness into His marvelous light (I Peter 2:9).

II. THE HUMILIATION OF SELF FOR SERVICE (12:3-8)

Once the self is put in right relationship to God, he is then ready to follow His will wherever it leads; and it will inevitably issue in service. But one thing is essential if he is to be used in service. He must make a proper evaluation of himself. This will always result in humility. An accurate inventory of self will bring a realization of gifts and the area where they can be used. Usually this brings recognition of limitations and weaknesses and consequent descent to that level where one can be used of the Lord.

A. Sober estimation of self is the initial impact of transformation (v. 3). Lest some imagine that the apostle is being officious he reminds them at the outset that this word of counsel is an act of grace. It is an approach to everyone in the Christian community. Self-exaltation bodes peril to the believer and to the cause of Christ. Conceit is a species of insanity that inducts folk into places and positions they are incapable of filling, and brings not only them to sorrow but also those whom they seek to serve. On the other hand a sober estimation is bound to result in the recognition of gifts imparted by God that properly equip them for special tasks. Sober estimation will not result in underestimation of the gifts of God, for this would only produce a false humility. But following the word of counsel, a sober estimation will always be measured by the faith that God has imparted to each one. This must mean that the proportion of gifts is measured by the ability to receive and use for Him.

B. The several members of the body of Christ point to the fact that there are differing performances within the body (vv. 4-5). The church is a body, a mystical body, formed by the operation of the Spirit of God (I Cor. 12:13). It takes many members to form the one body, but each member has a different function to perform, and all the functions are necessary to have a complete organism. But each member is vitally associated with every other member because they all share in the same life and are joined together in relation to the same Head (Eph. 1:22-23). The several members perform various functions under the direction of the Head, contributing benefit to each other and operating in perfect harmony. The preservation of the welfare of all in the spirit of harmony is essential guidance for those who are making a searching examination of themselves in order to serve.

C. Some of the spiritual gifts are now listed (vv. 6-8). They are gifts of grace, as the word means, which further means they are imparted without regard to any merit in the individual who possesses them. Elsewhere in Scripture other lists are given (I Cor. 12:4-11, 28-30; Eph. 4:11; I Peter 4:10). It is very possible that these lists are only representative. Certainly the Spirit is not limited in what He can impart to men. But in any event, there is no room for boasting on the part of the one who has been thus equipped. The list in these verses includes prophecy for revelation, ministry for edification, teaching for understanding, exhortation for stimulation, giving for welfare, ruling for administration, and mercy for comfort and need.

A word is added in relation to each gift, suggesting the way the gift should be exercised. Prophecy is to be exercised as measured by the proportion of faith. Though many expositors take this to mean the faith of the individual prophet, it is very possible that this means as measured by the general body of truth.[3] Even prophets needed some objective standard to guide them. Ministry should be a genuine effort to provide for the welfare of others. A teacher should be careful to impart understanding. The one who exhorts needs to fulfill his task by coming to the side of one and encouraging him. Giving is a great gift. But it should be exercised in such a way that there is simplicity—that is, with the absence of two-facedness. Diligence is a necessary quality for one who stands at the head of a group and rules. Mercy to be effective must be done with cheerfulness, hilarity, spontaneity, and abandonment.

3. W. H. Griffith Thomas, *The Devotional Commentary: Romans Vol. III* (London: The Religious Tract Society, n.d.), p. 25.

III. THE DEDICATION OF SELF TO OTHERS (12:9-21)

A. The principle of love is in itself the one necessary quality for the proper exercise of spiritual gifts (vv. 9, 10). A whole chapter is devoted to this theme in I Corinthians 13. Love seeks the good of its object and is in no sense hypocritical. It must separate itself from evil and seek only that which is good. Even though the love of verse 9 lays emphasis on counting the value of the brethren, verse 10 suggests that the saints go a step farther and find something attractive in each one and respond with warm affection, even to the point of giving others a place of ascendency over self.

B. At this point a whole list of virtues is encouraged (vv. 11-16). There should be no sluggishness in one's earnestness, but a zealousness of spirit in serving the Lord. Rejoicing ought to characterize the hope for the future, with persistence under pressure and steadfastness in prayer. There should be a sharing in the needs of the saints, pursuing the stranger to do him good, and blessing those who pursue you to do harm, blessing them and not cursing. There is an intense need for sympathy in the congregation of the saints. With those who are weeping, believers should weep; and where there are those who rejoice, saints should join them in rejoicing. There should be a oneness of mind among the saints. This should exclude a supercilious attitude and should include concern for those who are lowly. It is dangerous for a believer to isolate himself to his own counsels.

C. Paul now enlarges the responsibility of the believer beyond the Christian community (vv. 17-21). Reciprocation of evil for evil ought never to be experienced. Even though one may be moved to evil, as a Christian he ought to present everything in an honorable and beautiful way before men. There may be times when tranquility is impossible, but insofar as possible peacefulness should characterize the life of the believer with all men. Vengeance is not the prerogative of the saint. The place of anger belongs to the Lord, and in due time He will repay on a basis that is righteous and holy. The saints are bound to have enemies, but they should do them good rather than evil, for in some way this will be more of a judgment on them than evil. Let the believer follow the principle of Christ, which is to overcome evil with good.

All the above things will mark a transformation into the likeness of Christ and a turning from those things which belong to this present passing age.

Questions for Individual Study

1. How does the word "therefore" in verse 1 link the section that follows with the preceding one?
2. What is the meaning of the word "brethren," and how does this constitute an occasion for exhortation?
3. What are "the mercies of God," and how do these provide a basis for an appeal?
4. What does it mean to present the body a living sacrifice, and how is this reasonable?
5. What is transformation, and how is this accomplished?
6. What does it mean to think soberly of oneself, and what relation does this have to spiritual gifts?
7. What are some of the qualities that will characterize dedication of self to others?

Chapter 11

Transformation in Relation to Organized Government
Romans 13:1-14

The underlying and overruling principle of transformation in the life and conduct of the believer still continues. The will of God must be the guiding principle in transformation in all areas of life. The inward response of submission to the will of God must prevail in every detail and aspect of life if conduct on the part of the believer is to meet the qualifications for fulfilling "that good, and acceptable, and perfect, will of God" (12:2). This is also true for the believer as he confronts the government under which he lives.

This note was struck in the concluding words of the previous chapter (12:17-21), and the apostle now enlarges on the theme in relation to the outside world. Submission to the will of God requires that evil will never be demonstrated toward others. The ideal in exhibiting this principle took shape in the life and ministry of Christ. Nor should the believer take the prerogatives of government into his hands to execute vengeance. That right belongs alone to God, and God has delegated to civil government the right of inflicting retributive justice. The positive way for Christians to respond toward the wicked is with good. This good will accomplish more and will eventually overcome evil (12:17-21).

Nevertheless, government, in the sense of officially constituted authority, is very much a fact of life. On the human and natural level it is the prerogative of government to execute wrath on evildoers. And government in the ideal sense has carried out this responsibility over the years. The people of God have always been highly suspicious of the pressures that were exerted against them. Now Paul is writing to Christians living in the capital city of the Roman Empire. Nero Caesar is upon the throne, a man noted for his excesses against Christians, not only in Rome but across the empire. This has created a deep concern in the minds of most Christians, and without a doubt in the minds of Christians in Rome.

While it is true that Christians have been saved out of this world, they are living very much in this world and must confront certain civic and civil responsibilities. Just what relationship should the Christian sustain to the state? In the early church this was a very live issue. While on earth Jesus had announced that "my kingdom is not of this world" (John 18:36). He had called believers out of this world and had admonished them to be separated from the world. Yet in His high priestly prayer He had said, "I pray not that thou shouldest take them out of the world, but that thou shouldest keep them from the evil" (John 17:15). The seemingly conflicting lines of truth troubled the saints.

Inasmuch as the Christian is a citizen of the state as well as a member of the church, there was deep need for instruction on how to apply the principle of spiritual transformation in this dual capacity. In order to reconcile allegiance to Christ with allegiance to the state, the apostle devoted a whole chapter to the subject. In this chapter he puts the believer at ease with respect to the matter of nonresistance mentioned in the closing words of the previous chapter (12:19-21). To some it could appear that leaving vengeance wholly in the hands of the Lord could result in anarchy. But Paul hastens to point out that God has constituted civil authority for the purpose of controlling society.

Local circumstances must have provoked this reference to civil authority, in view of the fact that Paul seldom mentions the matter in his epistles (I Tim. 2:2). The Jews at Rome—as elsewhere thoughout the empire—were notorious for their insurgence. What they believed about their own position and theocracy made submission to Gentile authority almost intolerable (Deut. 17:14-17; Mark 12:13-17), and very recently they had rebelled and suffered expulsion from Rome (Acts 18:2). The close relation of Christians to Jews resulted in Christians being regarded as guilty of revolutionary tendencies. To prevent Christians from falling into the same pattern of response toward civil authority and to protect them from false accusation, the apostle now turns to a discussion of this important area of life and the proper relation of the Christian in seeking the will of God.[1]

There is a threefold movement in unfolding the thought of this chapter. The first is occupied with discussion of the relation of the Christian to the powers of the state (vv. 1-7). The second is concerned with the relation of the Christian to the people of the state (vv. 8-10). And the third is devoted to a discussion of the relation of the Christian to the prospect for the state (vv. 11-14). The first calls for obedience to the authority of the state. The second points to obligation toward the people of the state. And the third gives optimism in anticipation of change in the state.

I. THE RELATION TO THE POWER OF THE STATE (13:1-7)

Let us note three things that appear in the progressive unfolding of these verses: the ordination of the powers (vv. 1-2); the operation of these powers (vv. 3-4); and the obligation to obey these powers (vv. 5-7).

A. The ordination of the civil powers is an act performed by God (vv. 1-2). Organization, order, and arrangement is the chief point being made in the opening verses of this chapter. There is no area or aspect of the universe which is not characterized by order and arrangement, and this is also true of society (Eph. 1:11; Ps. 75:6-7; Dan. 4:25, 32; John 19:10-11).

1. *The proper arrangement of the believer under civil authority is enjoined upon every Christian* (v. 1a). The words "be subject" point to an arrangement or position underneath the person who has been delegated to a position of authority. This is

1. W. H. Griffith Thomas, *The Devotional Commentary: Romans Vol. III*, p. 49.

a command, the moral implications of which will be discussed later.

2. *The positional arrangement under God is true for all authorities* (v. 1b). There are cases in Old Testament history where God moved immediately to place certain men in positions of authority, such as Moses and David. But for the most part God has always operated providentially through society. Nevertheless, even in this case it is no less a fact that such men derive their authority from God and are under God.

3. *The perfected arrangement under God is a present fact with continuing force* (v. 1c). The verb "ordained" is in the perfect tense, pointing to an action in the past the force of which continues right up to the present. In the past these authorities were arranged under God, and they still retain that place, performing delegated responsibilities.

4. *Any personal arrangement against these authorities constitutes an act of standing against the imperial agreement made with these men* (v. 2a). The first "resisteth" means "to arrange against." It is a way of pointing out how a man destroys God's organization. The second "resisteth" means to take a stand against and thus become an adversary. He does that by taking a stand against the "ordinance," that is, the set of arrangements used by God to bring the official to his position. In a monarchy those arrangements may be by the line of succession. In a democracy it may be by election. But by whatever method the official comes to the place of authority, it is to be regarded as divine arrangement.

5. *Penal consequences are incurred by those who deliberately withstand the supreme authority* (v. 2b). "Damnation" refers to some sort of temporal judgment that the supreme authority may deem proper for committing this crime. The word does not refer to condemnation from God in the sense of being spiritually lost.

B. The operation of governmental authority is set forth in positive terms (vv. 3-4). But from this the negative is revealed by inference. "Subjection on the part of the believer is to be rendered to the power when he is fulfilling the true intent of his calling and office. If he violates that, then it is clearly the duty of the Christian in loyalty to God, to disobey him."[2] Early Christians found themselves in this situation (Acts 4:18-20; 5:28-29). Saints of Old Testament days too were sometimes confronted with this problem (Dan. 3:13-18). In the passage before us, however, Paul is setting forth under God the true intent of government.

1. *The purpose of God in government is twofold.* On the one hand it is for the protection of society (v. 3). In a world of sin where most people are not Christians there are bound to be evil works; and against these, human government is designed to impose fear. In this way the active government of God in human affairs provides for the welfare of society. On the other hand human government promotes the welfare of society (v. 4). The civil authority is a minister of good. There are innumerable projects involving organized society that could not be accomplished apart from the leadership and promotion of the government.

2. *The performance for God toward government should be displayed by the believer.* Recognizing the positive intent of government for good, the believer should therefore do good as unto God. Doing good not only brings the approval of God for the performance of His will, but in the light of the true intent of government there is no need for fear (v. 4). But on the other hand, if one deliberately ignores the true intent of government and does what is evil, then he justly has every reason to fear (v. 3).

3. *The praise of God through government will be the experience for those who do good* (v. 3). This does not mean that he will receive reward except in the sense of recognition on the part of

2. G. Campbell Morgan, *The Analyzed Bible: Romans,* pp. 206-7.

government for being a good man and contributing to the welfare of society. Joseph was such a man and came to the place of great influence in the land of Egypt (Gen. 39:12, 20-23; 41:38-41). Under Ahasuerus, King of Persia, Mordecai was honored (Esther 8:15), and Daniel under Nebuchadnezzar (Dan. 1:8-9).

4. *The penalty of God through government consists in the execution of wrath* (v. 4). This is the same wrath spoken of in 1:18. But in this case it is temporal and not final. Hence the purpose is to protect society from those who practice evil. In this sense the civil authority is a minister of God attending continually in the oversight of society. Most wicked men in the ultimate sense understand only one language—the language of physical force exhibited in the use of the sword. So this minister of God does not brandish the sword in vain. The purpose is to instill fear and hinder evil. When the penalty for evil works falls on men in organized society the government is serving as a revenger, that is, the executor of that which comes out of righteousness or justice, a responsibility delegated to men by God. Justice on the human and natural level may fall far short of what God would perform immediately; but it is nevertheless a form of justice without which the world of organized society would lapse into anarchy, confusion, violence, and terror. On more than one occasion the apostle Paul himself appealed to civil authority for protection (Acts 18:12-17; 19:35-41; 22:25). And the instances where the interests of the people of God have been protected and promoted by civil authority are without number.

C. The obligation for Christians to obey civil authorities is clearly set forth in Scripture (vv. 5-7). It is understood that this applies when government is performing its true intent under God, either on the one hand to promote the welfare of society or on the other to protect society from evil-workers.

1. *The compulsion for submission to civil authority is twofold* (v. 5). The first that comes to mind for most people is that of prudence in fear of consequences. Men are so made that they first evaluate the implications of failure to abide by the law of the

land as administered by civil authorities. For Christians this is the lesser of the reasons for arranging themselves under constituted authority. The second and primary reason is principle issuing from the conscience. Conscience is that function in moral beings that brings together the twofold aspect of reality. There is knowledge on the one hand of God in His relation to civil authority. And on the other there is the relation of the believer to God. Since it is God who has established the civil authority, then the willing response of the believer should be submission to what God has ordained.

2. *The completion of submission is the bearing of the burden of taxation* (v. 6a). It is rather interesting that the word "tribute" or tax translates into the word which essentially means "burden." This means that even in Paul's day taxes were viewed as burden. But this burden was an essential burden. It was for the purpose of supporting the government, for which in turn there were benefits to the citizenry. The word "pay" points to the completion or fulfillment of something. In this case it means that a man has not completed his act of subordination to government until he has paid his taxes. Christians performed this responsibility like others with a sense of fear. But how much more appropriate for them to fulfill this responsibility with the realization that it is being done as unto God and in the knowledge that the taxation is helping to create the benefits which they receive from government (Matt. 17:27).

3. *The civil servant in submission is steadfastly performing his duties for the welfare of society* (v. 6b). The word "minister" in this verse differs from that in verse 4. The first word was more general. This one describes him as a public or sacred servant. More literally he is a worker for the people. The Old Testament priests were such (Heb. 8:2), and Christ Himself, our high priest, is such a minister (Heb. 8:6). Civil servants are often men who give themselves to public office out of a sense of duty to society for little or no pay. The responsibilities continue around the clock and demand a tremendous outlay of energy and patience.

But steadfastly and with diligence they perform their tasks, many of them little realizing that they are actually ministers in the service of God in relation to society.

4. *The command for submission follows as a logical outcome for Christians* (v. 7). The word "dues" points to a moral obligation. In view of the fact that the civil servant is God's minister, the believer is morally obligated to subordinate himself as to God. It is rank blasphemy for a Christian to claim submission to God on the one hand and then to rebel against God's servant on the other. This is proper so long as the civil servant performs the true intent of his delegated authority. If there is failure at this point, then there is doubtless room for protest, but certainly in the right way. Since no type or form of government is mentioned, this becomes a principle that may be followed by Christians under any form of government. Care should be taken always to consider the benefits provided by the civil authority.

Every type of public servant and every aspect of moral obligation is enjoined on the believer. He should pay tribute to whom tribute is due, recognizing that the support of government is essential for the creation of benefits for society. He should not hesitate to pay custom where it is levied. Toll on goods brings certain benefits in return. Fear or respect for authority is essential for the well-being of society and helps to create an atmosphere of tranquility. Honor is that recognition of value in public servants. It is compensation of the highest sort—a compensation which no amount of money can supplant.

II. THE RELATION TO THE PEOPLE OF THE STATE (13:8-10)

In addition to responsibility to the civil authorities, for the Christian there are responsibilities to the citizens of the state. He must live and move among them, and he ought to bear his testimony to them. For this group he will be able to conscript members for the church.

A. The obligation to the citizens of the state is first stated in general terms (v. 8). It is that of love—not a mere sentimental or emotional expression, but a love that recognizes value in people and seeks to communicate benefit. On the negative side this means that one ought not to owe any man anything. Owing means that one has experienced benefit provided by someone else and of which that man is presently deprived. Withholding what belongs to another is certainly not seeking to do that person good. So Christians ought not to owe anything.

But Christians are obligated to pursue a path of owing and paying *love* to others. There can never be a time when the believer has finished paying this debt. In that moment when a man ceases to owe his neighbor love he will begin to be in debt in some other direction. The constant consciousness of the believer is that love to his neighbor is always due even though it is constantly being paid.[3] In this sense love is the fulfilling of the law for those who walk not after the flesh but after the spirit.

B. The opportunities for expressing love are outlined in some detail in the law (v. 9). The believer ought not to defraud others in the area of purity such as adultery, nor in the area of life such as murder, nor in the area of property such as stealing, nor in the area of truth such as false witness, nor in the area of possession such as coveting. One statement of the law covers a wide range of social relationships, namely, "Thou shalt love thy neighbor as thyself."

C. The outcome of life in relation to the citizens of the state consists in the fulfillment of the law (v. 10). It is the very nature of love to seek the good of its object, and this in turn excludes the working of ill. It is then that love becomes in the fullest sense the fulfillment of the law. Love is a motivating force that proceeds from within and cannot be generated from without. It is not response to compulsion from without. It is abandonment to the will of God evidenced to the outside world by living relationships to men.

3. Morgan, p. 209.

III. IN RELATION TO THE PROSPECT FOR THE STATE (13:11-14)

The state is far from perfect, no matter whether you look at the civil authorities or the citizens of the state. Christians feel as pilgrims passing through and as strangers in a foreign land. The imperfections, the vices, the wickedness, the oppression are enough to fill the heart of the Christian with fear and induce him to seek flight from these scenes. But something better lies ahead. The present scenes are temporary and passing, and shortly the King of kings and the Lord of lords will come and establish the final and perfect order. His kingdom will cover the earth and will be characterized by absolute righteousness. Upon this hope Paul now centers the attention of the believer.

A. The time for the passing of the present state and the ushering in of the new one is at hand (v. 11). The apostle emphasizes this fact by bringing the time progressively nearer. He starts out with the word for *time* which means "season" or "proper time." He moves to the words "high time" which is a translation of the word *hour*. Then he dares to use the word "now." These words for time dictate conduct. "Sleep" pictures the person in prostrate position and in a state of inactivity. The word "awake" is actually the word for "rise" or "raise" and points to an upright position and being in a state of activity. Since the future aspect of salvation is nearer than when we believed, this is the proper time for energetic performance.

B. The day of the Lord which is to follow the long night of sin has drawn near (v. 12). Nineteen centuries ago the apostle Paul insisted that the night of sin had made such progress toward the end that it was about to conclude. The night of sin and sorrow and sighing is about over. What a welcome sound that must have been to the saints in Rome. But if that night was well on its way then, think of how near its end is today. The day of the Lord is about to dawn. This means that everything that belongs to the night should be cast off. Night clothes, the works of darkness, should be put off. In place of them the believer ought to put on the armor of light so he is prepared for the activity of the day.

C. The walk for the believer should take on all the qualities that make it beautiful and attractive (vv. 13-14). Of necessity this means that the sins which characterize night life should be abandoned. This includes the sins of intemperance such as rioting and drunkenness, the sins of impurity such as chambering and wantonness, and the sins of immaturity such as strife and envying. On the positive side believers should put on the Lord Jesus Christ. This will mean temperance, purity, and maturity—maturity always producing the flower of love. These positive fruits will of necessity exclude from time and place the mental involvement of plans for the flesh and the satisfaction of its lusts. This will be adequate preparation for that kingdom where everything is holiness unto the Lord (Zech. 14:20-21).

Questions for Individual Study

1. Why did the apostle make a transition from the subject of transformation to that of the state?
2. Is there real need for the Christian to be instructed about his attitude and conduct toward the state?
3. What relationship does civil authority have to God? And what should be the response of Christians?
4. What twofold purpose of God is delegated to civil government?
5. For what two reasons ought the Christian to obey the powers? Which is the higher reason?
6. What should be the relationship of the believer to the citizens of the state?
7. Why does Paul point the believer to the coming of the Lord? Does this bear on the subject of the state?

Chapter 12

Transformation in Relation to Christian Fellowship
Romans 14:1-23

From the opening of the Book of Romans to its close there is a continuous flow of thought. One area of discussion merges into another as the theological treatise unfolds. The logical and literary connections are either understood or expressed to establish the relationships of thought. In moving from chapter 13 to chapter 14 the connection is expressed. It is amazing, however, how many versions omit the connection. The English Revised Version and the American Standard Version both render the Greek connective into English by the word *but.*

The Greek connective is adversative in sense but only slightly so. It points to the fact that the story moves on, but there is a slight contrast in the material. This would seem to indicate that the general matters being treated in chapters 12 and 13 are now concluded and the apostle turns to matters that are more specific. Nevertheless, he continues to apply the law of love in the relationships of the believer as evidence of transformation in pursuit of the will of God. He has treated the matter of transformation in relation to individual life and in relation to the state. Now he touches on transformation in relation to Christian fellowship.

The church was a new society of believers. Into its membership came people from all walks of life, from all nationalities, and out of various cultures and religions. Every sort of personality was represented, and the saints were in every stage of Christian development. With the imperfections of sin manifest in each one, all these features combined to produce problems. One of these problems had to do with the meaning and latitude of Christian liberty. The apostle Paul had already confronted this problem in Corinth and devoted three chapters of his first epistle to the discussion of it (I Cor. 8—10).

It seems quite apparent that he anticipated this problem among the saints in Rome. There were Jews as well as Gentiles in that church. The Jew had a background of centuries in following a strict code dealing with sacred days and specific diets. This developed in him a strong devotion to scruples. But for the Gentile who was saved out of idolatry, it is possible that he was able to shake off the influence of former life. However, this may not necessarily be so, as can be seen by reference to the problems in the Corinthian church in this area. Varying personalities and different stages of Christian growth could produce the same thing.

Two different stages of Christian growth are specifically mentioned. There is the brother who is "weak in the faith" (14:1) and those "that are strong" (15:1). By the use of the word "weak" the apostle does not mean to imply that these people are morally weak. Quite the opposite is true. They are morally very scrupulous. The brother who is "strong" is not to be understood as being morally scrupulous. It is very possible that he is quite the opposite. The believer who is "weak" is "weak in the faith." This means he does not comprehend the full meaning of the faith he has espoused. On the contrary, the "strong" brother is one who does understand the Christian faith and has entered into its freedom.

The real issue between these two brothers was the failure of each to appreciate the position of the other. Here was a place where there was need for instruction and especially a place for the exercise of love. Here was a place where the strong brother needed to learn how to show Christian consideration for the weak saint. This was also the place where the weak brother needed to learn esteem and toleration. Until some common ground was found for mutual concern, Christian fellowship could not live and prosper. To this problem the apostle now addresses himself. The first half of this chapter is a discussion of consideration expressing itself in mutual permission (vv. 1-12).

The final half of the chapter deals with consideration expressing itself in mutual edification (vv. 13-23).

I. CONSIDERATION AND MUTUAL PERMISSION (14:1-12)

An examination of this passage reveals three things: the problems gathered about certain matters, the mention of certain principles for solving the problems, and the various provisions serving as incentives for action.

A. The problems gathered about questions concerning diet and observance of days (vv. 2-6). This was inevitable inasmuch as the congregation was made up of both Jews and Gentiles.

1. *Diet was a most significant issue in the early church* (vv. 2-3). The background of Judaism out of which Jews came had strict laws governing the diet. There were clean and unclean animals. The unclean were forbidden to the Jew (Acts 10:11-14). Because of the background of the Gentile there were problems about things offered to idols (I Cor. 8:4). Beyond these there were even greater refinements in the problem. There were some who could eat everything and were without scruples with respect to the flesh of animals. Still others limited themselves severely to a vegetarian diet.

2. *Days in the calendar set aside for special purposes concerned many* (vv. 5-6). One believer would attach special significance to one day and lift it above all the other days of the week, month, or year. This was true in Jewry. The Sabbath day called for special recognition. There were special feast days that were differentiated from other days. These even had the authority of God upon them. Naturally these carried over into the Christian era. Even the first day of the week came to have special significance because Christ rose on that day. Through all these centuries this sacredness continues. But there were others in the Christian family who treated every day alike. Strong convictions, deep feelings, and many intricacies combined to make this a very sensitive situation.

B. The principles for guiding in the solution to these problems strike at the heart of the Christian faith (vv. 1, 3, 5, 6).

1. *The strong believer is urged to respond with loving reception of the weak brother* (v. 1). As you can see, it is the strong Christian who is addressed, even though the word "strong" does not appear until chapter 15 and verse 1. Really, this is a high compliment. It is evidence that the apostle realized that the proper approach is to begin with that believer who is farthest along on the road to spiritual maturity. Since he is the one who has knowledge and is the one who claims to understand, then he is the one who is most apt to be able to receive the instruction the apostle is about to give. He is admonished to "receive," meaning in this place to welcome to his company and into a face-to-face relationship of equality and fellowship, that saint who is weak in the faith. He is further admonished not to do this with the intent of engaging him in debate or of casting doubt or reflection on him. There should be no effort to expose his ignorance or contest his opinions. It means that strong Christians are not to sit in judgment on the scruples of their weak brethren.[1] The strong believer is urged to make a free, open, gracious welcome of the weak brother, giving him equal standing and unfettered fellowship. Difficulties are not to be discussed. Doubts are not to be suggested. Discrimination is not to be entertained.

2. *In matters of diet both types of Christians are urged to show mutual permission for the conduct of the other* (v. 3). The strong brother who feels perfectly free in eating anything he desires should not "despise" or look down on that weak brother who scrupulously abstains from eating certain things. The word "despise" carries strong connotations. It means to treat as nothing and therefore to regard with contempt. In the face of such an attitude and in such an atmosphere the weak brother could find it almost impossible to exist. This could drive him from the

1. W. H. Griffith Thomas, *The Devotional Commentary: Romans Vol. III*, pp. 73-74.

Christian assembly and thus lay the groundwork for division. If God smiles on the weak brother and has graciously received him with high approval, then certainly the strong brother should be able to make provision in his thinking for the extreme sensitivities of the weak brother.

On the other hand the weak brother is admonished about his attitude and conduct toward the strong brother. Because the strong brother feels perfectly free to eat food that the weak brother feels belongs on the black list, the weak brother should not take this as an occasion for censorious criticism of the strong. He should not carry in his thinking a low view of the discernment of the strong and a deep sense of wounded sanctity in his bosom. He should try to realize that the strong brother is acting from pure motives and that only God can rightly evaluate them. In this case God has been gracious in welcoming this brother to Himself and He completely ignores those matters of such high sensitivity to the weak brother in receiving the strong into fellowship. If God has received the strong brother into complete and untrammeled fellowship, then certainly the weak brother can do no less.

3. Moreover, believers should understand that each Christian has personal responsibility to God (vv. 5-6). It is therefore important that each Christian, strong or weak, be persuaded in his own mind as to the rightness or the wrongness of his conduct. This places the matter in the realm of conscience. On the one hand conscience will dictate what is right as God lays down restrictions. And on the other it will tell the individual believer how he measures up to the restriction. In this persuasion the believer should order his conduct, for this is unto God.

The strong believer may find that his conscience in the presence of God makes full provision for the eating of any food without restriction. Then let him eat after this fashion in full freedom and with clear conscience. He may be persuaded that there is no difference in days. To him every day is alike, and he must regard every day as a day when he should be serving the Lord. Every day is sacred and life is to be lived the same way

through every day of life. If this is the conclusion of his conscience, then he ought to live just that way.

But the weak brother may be convinced otherwise as to days
and diet. Because of the association of idolatry Daniel was com-
pelled to restrict himself in matters of diet (Dan. 1:8, 12). It could
be that Sabbath observance led Christians to transfer strict oversight to the first day of the week, Sunday, feeling that it must be
set aside from all the other days of the week. As the reader of this
account well knows, there are today strong feelings among
many Christians that Sunday should be set aside in distinction
from all other days of the week. Paul is therefore saying, if this be
the case, then let a man follow the conviction of his heart; for that
conviction is the thing that binds him to God.

C. Certain provisions are called to the attention of believers
(vv. 4, 7-11). These provide incentives to usher the principles
into operation. It will be seen that these principles reach deep
into the life and ministry of Christ.

1. *The present work of Christ in the believer is essentially the
source from which the believer derives strength to stand* (v. 4).
Each believer is the servant of Christ. What person has the right
to evaluate another man's servant? The answer to that is clear: no
one. The slavery of that day made this perfectly clear to everyone. On a higher level it is just as true. It is the master of that
servant who alone has the right to evaluate his service. If the
master feels that it is inferior, he can reprimand him. If the
master feels that it is superior, he can commend him. In either
case the master will uphold him. A servant was bound to the
master for life; and even if he failed to do his best, the master did
not fire him. He retained him and initiated such means to bring
his service up to commendable level. In the same way, and far
beyond what any earthly master could do, Christ works in His
servants to perform all the good pleasure of His will (Phil. 2:13).
Paul had found in his own experience that he could do all things
because Christ worked in him to strengthen him (Phil. 4:13).

2. *The past work of Christ with its continuing force provided*

for the whole experience of the believer (vv. 7-9). Living and
dying comprehends the whole realm of experience in the existence of the believer. Living is never done by itself, nor is dying
experienced by itself, nor are these two areas of experience
confined to the believer himself. Living is unto the Lord and
dying is also unto the Lord. Whether we live or die, both experiences are unto the Lord. After all, believers are the servants of the
Lord. He follows intimately and minutely all the details that go
to make up the activity of His servant. And when that servant
dies, no one is more concerned than the Lord, for one of His
servants has been taken out of activity. Like no other master,
Christ was able to go through all the experiences His servants
will go through in order that He might in the fullest sense be
Lord of both the dead and the living. When Christ died He
purchased believers for Himself and they now belong to Him.
When He rose and lived He conquered death so that He is now
able to bring His servants out of the realm of death. In the most
absolute sense He is Lord. Even those who have passed on
belong to Him, and in His time He will bring them forth from the
grave.

3. *The future work of Christ will bring to completion and
permanence the lordship of Christ over His servants* (vv. 10-12).
There is a day coming when the entire Christian brotherhood
will stand before the judgment seat of Christ where their service
will be evaluated. This evaluation will cover all that they have
done as Christians. It will include the attitudes they have shown
toward their Christian brethren. It is then that the Great Master
will hand out the rewards of commendation for work well done,
or the reproofs for service that has been inferior. In view of this
coming examination it behooves believers to exercise unusual
reticence and holy fear for what lies ahead. Contempt for the
weak brother when exposed to the white light of God's evaluation may prove to be something faulty, inaccurate, and most
reprehensible. Censorious criticism of the strong brother may
not only prove to be absolutely wrong, but it may also uncover a
wicked and hateful heart in the weak brother. This exposure will

call for confession on the part of strong and weak alike. How much better to consider the issues now and avoid the embarrassing exposure of the future. Assuming the place of judge now will be supplanted by bowing the knee then. Any cherished conceit of right judgment now will be replaced by confession then. The infallible Scripture asserts this (Isa. 45:23). This rests on the fact that responsibility now will someday at the judgment seat of Christ be confronted with accountability to God who is the absolute, final, and just judge of all.

II. CONSIDERATION AND MUTUAL EDIFICATION (14:13-23)

Whereas the preceding argument was in a sense negative, or at least neutral, so far as solving the problems between the strong and the weak, the argument from this point on takes on a more positive character. No longer is the emphasis on mere mutual permission. It now assumes the necessity of mutual edification. There are certain things that are essential for the building up of the body of Christ.

A. Certain principles governing personal conduct must be inculcated in the lives of believers (vv. 13-15). Apart from these the Christian fellowship will fail.

1. *There should be concern for the spiritual state of one another* (v. 13). This is a call to abdicate the throne of judgment against one another, and in its place to explore how one can make a contribution to or remove a hindrance from his brother's progress in the Christian life. This calls for introspection. It calls for an evaluation of self as to the assistance he may be providing for his spiritual welfare.

2. *There should be concern for the spiritual standards of one another* (v. 14). When intrinsic and essential worth is considered, there is nothing in the realm of creation that God did not pronounce good (Gen. 1:31). This can only mean that it is the attitude and use to which things are put that makes things unclean. Since this is true, then it is wise and proper and good

for believers to respect the attitudes of one another. Some will set a standard for themselves one way, and it does not change the essence of things. Others will set another standard, and that attitude does not change the quality of things.

3. *There should be concern for the spiritual servantship of one another* (v. 15). This is reference again to the law of love. If eating meat causes a brother to stumble and fall, the issue of which is destruction, then there is really no concern for the value of that man. Christ placed such a high value on that man that He died to save him. Is it possible that a believer for the sake of his own selfish attitude on food would actually counteract the work of Christ and contribute to the destruction of a believer? This is certainly not the law of love that motivated the ministry of Christ.

B. The importance of the preservation of personal testimony cannot be overlooked as a means of accomplishing the purpose of Christ (vv. 16-18). No matter how much one knows about the truth, nor how right he may be in his conduct in relation to things that are not wrong in themselves, he may endanger his testimony with the weak brother by the doing of them. For this reason he needs to be reminded of some things.

1. *Personal testimony is important* (v. 16). A believer ought not to permit the good thing he is doing to be held up to ridicule as evil, if it lies within his power to avoid it. An attitude of "I don't care what people think" is wrong in itself. It does matter what people think, and what they think can be controlled by the discipline of self without any loss to self. The responsibility to act in that way before God is inescapable.

2. *The essential nature of the kingdom is spiritual* (v. 17). This means that the Holy Spirit controls and exercises dominion over the kingdom. Even where matters of material things (such as food and drink) are concerned, the Holy Spirit controls that. The ultimate purpose and atmosphere of the kingdom is a spiritual control that issues in righteousness, peace, and joy. Any attitude

or conduct in the use of material things that destroys this purpose is not of the Spirit.

3. *The divine sovereignty of Christ is at stake* (v. 18). If the line of authority for each believer is traced directly to Christ, his conduct will be acceptable to God and it will be approved by men. "This is the true attitude of the genuine man of God, and the life thus lived with constant regard to helpfulness to our fellow-Christians will have the twofold effect of being acceptable to God and approved by men. Such a life will stand the supreme test of divine examination."[2]

C. The purpose of God may be completely fulfilled by abstention from the eating of certain foods on the one hand, or the participation in them on the other (vv. 19-21).

1. *Edification of a Christian brother should be a primary concern in guiding the conduct of a Christian* (v. 19). Whether one is strong or weak, he should direct his life into a channel that will build up his brother in the faith and promote an atmosphere of peace.

2. *Destruction as a goal should be immediately ruled out* (v. 20). Food should not be made a priority in conduct either by abstention or participation. It is the welfare of a brother that is at stake—welfare not merely in the present, but his eternal welfare. There is nothing impure about food. But where the attitude of a brother enters into the picture, a true saint ought to be willing to forgo for his sake.

3. *Abstinence is perfectly good and is worthy of pursuit when a Christian brother's welfare is at stake* (v. 21). Certainly self-denial at a time like this takes on the qualities of attractiveness. In the final analysis, the failure to eat certain foods will not result in starvation. The only possible value in eating would be for a moment's physical satisfaction. The willingness to forgo dis-

2. Thomas, p. 84.

plays an inner quality that is winsome. But, then, participation may be possible.

D. The matter of personal persuasion becomes the final test for conduct in these various matters (vv. 22-23). In these last two verses the apostle points to a measuring rod for both the strong and the weak.

1. The strong brother is counseled to regard his own faith as a reason for prohibition (v. 22). In matters of faith, he may have full understanding concerning the things he is doing, and be convinced they are not wrong. But his faith is not something for him to put on display and boast about. His faith is something that is very intimate and personal and should be kept for himself and for God. In his conduct he will demonstrate that he is a blessed man if he does not pronounce a judgment against himself in that area of conduct in which he is being tested. This could mean and ought to mean that he will not eat foods or perform on days that will offend the weak brother.

2. The weak brother should be encouraged by his own faith to participate in certain things (v. 23). Discrimination in foods brings self-condemnation when there is participation. This is the law of conscience. It means that he eats without being persuaded that it is right. But if he could forsake that attitude for the moment and commit himself entirely into the hands of Christ, perhaps he could eat without the pangs of conscience. In any event, whatever one does without being persuaded that it is right is sin. Above all things, follow this dictum to the very end. The violation of conscience introduces serious issues into the principle of guidance for daily life.

Questions for Individual Study

1. What was there about the membership of the church that provided a background for the problems dealt with in chapter 14?
2. What were two of the problems in this area that came in for special mention in this chapter?

3. What is the meaning of the first verse of the chapter on the matter of reception?
4. What light does personal responsibility to the Lord throw on the solution to this problem?
5. If all things are good in themselves, what is it that makes them either good or evil as men look at them?
6. Where does personal testimony enter into the solution of problems on Christian liberty?
7. What is the final test for the conduct of weak and strong in relation to these matters?

Chapter 13

Transformation in Personal Contribution

Romans 15:1–16:24

The flow of thought initiated in chapter 12 moves on to its conclusion in chapters 15 and 16. It is concerned with transformation into the likeness of Christ according to the will of God. The theme began with transformation in individual living in relation to God (chap. 12). It then moved to transformation in political alignments (chap. 13). It proceeded to transformation in Christian fellowship (chap. 14). Now the apostle is ready to deal with transformation as it relates to personal contribution in life.

Once the central affirmation is made at the opening of this section (12:1-2), there is no break in the movement of thought to the end of the epistle. Two facts make this certain. The first grows out of the internal and intrinsic thought that runs through this section. One plateau of reasoning merges with and rises to the succeeding plateau until the concluding and crowning plateau is reached. Second, grammatical connectives are inserted into the original text to carry the reader forward in unbroken thought. In the King James Version these connectives were ignored by the translators so far as insertion into the English translation. These connectives make it clear that the writer is continuing the narrative though there is slight contrast in the content. But the contrast does not mean a change of subject matter, only a transition to another phase of the same theme (see 14:1; 15:1, 14; 16:1, 17, 25—Greek de).

These grammatical connectives along with the subject matter establish the fact that chapters 15 and 16 are integral parts of the Epistle to the Romans and that they appear in the proper place in the epistle. Tampering with the text in copying and transmission is conclusively offset by internal evidence of subject matter and the abundance of external evidence in manuscripts to establish the fact that the Epistle to the Romans does not conclude with chapter 14, but goes on to the end of chapter 16. Even the mention of the many personalities of chapter 16 does not militate against its authenticity as belonging to the epistle, but rather supports its right to a place in this epistle.

The great argument of the epistle is now drawing to a close. The writer is just ready to conclude this teaching on the out-working of the gospel in the lives of believers. He has laid a firm foundation for the final appeal for personal contribution in Christian life. For those who have entered into experience of the gospel and its saving grace, they are now equipped for service. They are responsible to realize transformation into the likeness of Christ according to the will of God (12:1-2). This should be the experience of every believer in individual living (chap. 12), in political alignments (chap. 13), and in Christian fellowship (chap. 14). But more than that, above and beyond what he has already called to their attention, transformation should take place in personal contribution to the cause of Christ. That is the burden of chapters 15 and 16.

The message of chapter 14 was directed primarily to the strong Christian. Even though here and there in the chapter admonition is directed to the weak brother, the bulk of the message is intended for the strong Christian. This follows the pattern of Paul's message in chapters 8-10 of I Corinthians. In those chapters the strong believer is instructed to use Christian liberty in relation to salvation (chap. 8), in relation to service (chap. 9), and in relation to spirituality (chap. 10). Pursuing that same pattern, Paul continues with the theme introduced in chapter 14. At the very outset of chapter 15 he addresses the strong and identifies himself with them. Upon them he lays a special burden, one that is commensurate with the level of Christian experience to which they have attained.

The key to chapters 15 and 16 is very clearly that of ministry.

The words "minister," "service," or some word carrying the same meaning are used often in these two chapters (15:8, 16, 25, 27, 31; 16:1, 3, 6, 12, 18). In fact these two chapters are permeated with the idea of ministry. Chapter 16, which on its surface seems to be occupied with other matters, actually breathes the atmosphere of ministry. Ministry is held up as the highest point of Christian experience. It is giving out of that which Christ has wrought within. It stands at the opposite pole from self-serving. It is self-sacrifice like that of Christ. Three movements of thought unfold in this division of the epistle: first, personal contribution and the ministry of Christ (15:1-13); second, personal contribution and the ministry of Paul (15:14-33); third, personal contribution and the ministry of saints (16:1-24).

I. PERSONAL CONTRIBUTION AND THE MINISTRY OF CHRIST (15:1-13)

Paul begins at the top. He holds up the ideal in Christ for ministry. "According to Christ Jesus" is the ideal rule of measure when appealing to believers for transformation into the likeness of Christ in personal contribution (15:5). Two qualities should characterize this ministry. The first is discussed in verses 1-6, that of goodness. The second is discussed in verses 7-13, that of glory to God.

A. The goodness of this ministry should truly be directed toward others, like that of Christ (vv. 1-6).

1. *There is an obligation that rests on strong believers to bear the infirmities of the weak* (vv. 1-2). The word "ought" translates the Greek word pointing to a moral obligation. Inasmuch as the strong claim to have more knowledge and comprehension, then it follows that they have greater responsibility. That greater light teaches that those who are the more able are morally obligated to bear the infirmities of those who lack the spiritual ability to perform as they ought. This does not mean to forbear, but to help carry the weak. This means that the chief concern should not be

the pleasing of self, but the pleasing of the weak neighbor to the end of doing him good in the sense of building him up in the Christian faith.

2. *There is an object lesson in Christ for the believer to follow* (vv. 3-4). Our Savior and Lord did not please Himself, though of all persons He not only had the right as sovereign, but also the purest of motives. Scripture clearly demonstrates that the reproaches of the wicked directed against God, which in turn made them liable to retribution, Christ voluntarily took upon Himself so that retributive wrath fell on Him (Ps. 69:9). In a very real sense He was made sin for us who knew no sin, that we might be made the righteousness of God in Him (II Cor. 5:21). "Who his own self bare our sins in his own body on the tree, that we, being dead to sins, should live unto righteousness" (I Peter 2:24). Paul's commentary on the purpose of Scripture is very much in point. The picture of self-sacrificing love which was at last completely fulfilled in Christ brings into bold relief the validity of Scripture and in turn the enlightenment it provides for perseverance and comfort. This means that the path of self-sacrificing love leads to a final triumph, and therefore energizes the heart with hope.

3. *The ultimate origin of true endurance and comfort comes from God; so the apostle addresses a prayer to God in behalf of believers* (vv. 5-6). The reason God is the absolute source lies in the fact that God is Himself characterized by endurance and consolation. Through the Holy Spirit who dwells within believers He can stir up or cultivate these qualities so that they demonstrate like-mindedness toward one another as measured over the pattern of Christ (Phil. 2:5-8). This means that they will not only think alike toward one another, but they will make profession of lips to this like-mindedness, and for no selfish glory. It will be to the glory of God just as Christ did in His sacrificial ministry. As one expositor explains:

> The use of the word "endurance," which always implies difficulty, to describe our treatment of weaker brethren, and the example of Christ under raillery of the enemies of God, reminds us how difficult it sometimes is to act towards weaker

brethren in a spirit of love. Our Christian character is seldom
so severely tried as when we are put to inconvenience by the
spiritual childishness of members of the church.[1]

**B. The glory of this ministry should find its ultimate goal in
God the Father as did the ministry of Christ** (vv. 7-13).

1. *The occasion for the appeal that is now addressed to the
saints is expressed in the opening word of verse 7.* It is the word
"wherefore," meaning "on account of which." This refers back
to the preceding paragraph and a ministry of goodness in bearing the infirmities of the weaker brethren. In performing this
ministry of goodness there should be that compelling motive of
bringing glory to God. The goodness of preserving a harmonious
unity within the Christian fellowship must have a destination
that reaches beyond the mere human and natural goal if it is to
possess its highest motivation and serve its largest purpose. For
the purpose of bringing glory to God a strong brother can overcome some of the most insurmountable obstacles in his weaker
brethren, just as Christ did when He received us to Himself to the
glory of God.

2. *The object lesson in Christ provides the pattern for conduct
on the part of the members of the church* (vv. 8-12). By means of a
very inconspicuous transition, the apostle moves from the
strong and weak brother to the Jew and Gentile (vv. 8-9). This
may have been in his mind all along, but he sought to lay a
foundation before making the transition. But in this transition
he returns to the theme he left in 11:32. The ministry of Christ
was to perform a particular function, that of being a minister of
the circumcision. Even though this is the only place in the New
Testament where this precise statement is made, there are other
places where Christ made it clear that He was sent to the lost
sheep of the house of Israel (Matt. 15:24; cf. 10:6). This con-
centration on Jews was for the truth of God with a twofold
purpose: first, to confirm the promises given to the fathers; and

1. J. Agar Beet, *St. Paul's Epistle to the Romans,* pp. 344-45.

second, that the Gentiles might glorify God for His mercy.[2] In His wise and perfect plan He sought out Israel first, that He might finally reach the Gentiles.

For confirmation of the point the apostle is now making, he marshals a body of truth from Scripture (vv. 9-12). Four passages are selected from the Old Testament to prove the universality of the gospel and the unity of Jew and Gentile within the church. The division which God effected when He called Abraham out from among the Gentiles, He has now canceled. This was long contemplated as indicated by these Old Testament passages (Deut. 32:43; Ps. 18:49; 117:1; Isa. 11:10). Since this distinction has been canceled as a dividing force in the program of God, believers should refuse to allow differences to cause divisions. This response on the part of believers will be to the glory of God.

3. *The outcome in the ultimate sense rests with the God of Hope* (v. 13). This is the only place where this expression is used. The only basis for hope is in a God who inspires hope, gives hope, and crowns hope with fulfillment. In anticipation of fulfillment He can fill the believer with joy and peace by exercising faith so that he will be filled with hope. This is ministered to the believer through the power of the indwelling Spirit. Thus mutual consideration and fellowship on the part of Jew and Gentile in the church of God promote the glory of God. "The Gentiles must remember that Christ became a Jew to save them; the Jews that Christ came among them in order that all the families of the earth might be blessed."[3] The aim is to promote God's glory.

II. PERSONAL CONTRIBUTION AND THE MINISTRY OF PAUL (15:14-33)

To bring the pattern of truth nearer to these people in Rome, the apostle now describes his own ministry. From the moment of

2. W.H. Griffith Thomas, *The Devotional Commentary: Romans Vol. III,* p. 100.
3. Sanday and Headlam, *International Critical Commentary: Romans,* p. 397.

his call into ministry and his assignment to the Gentiles he has not lost any opportunities to preach the gospel to them. Four outstanding qualities characterize this ministry: it is a particular ministry (vv. 14-17), a powerful ministry (vv. 18-21), a purposeful ministry (vv. 22-29), and a prayerful ministry (vv. 30-33).

A. A particular ministry was committed to Paul for discharge among Gentiles (vv. 14-17). As he looked at this ministry it meant several things.

1. *His persuasion was that Gentile Christians are true saints of God,* filled with goodness, filled with all knowledge, and able to admonish one another (v. 14). By this he meant they were fully equipped for service.

2. *His prerogative had specially to do with Gentiles* (v. 15). Acting boldly on that prerogative he did not hesitate to write them and put them in remembrance of some things. This right was his by virtue of the grace of God given to him.

3. *His passion in ministry was that he might be able to offer* up *the Gentiles as acceptable to God* (v. 16). Therefore he preached the gospel of God to the end that these saints might be sanctified and set aside from sin.

4. *His privilege in this ministry was finally to boast in Christ Jesus* (v. 17). This boasting had nothing of self involved. For this ministry among the Gentiles was given by sovereign grace, and it operated solely within the sphere and experience of grace.

B. A powerful ministry was carried forward by the apostle Paul among the Gentile nations (vv. 18-21).

1. *Permission was granted by the Lord Jesus Christ for him to preach among the Gentiles* (v. 18). He feels that in this area alone he has the right to speak. But this is enough. It meant that his words and deeds had been effectively used of the Lord to make the Gentiles obedient to the gospel.

2. *Power was especially manifested in his ministry* (v. 19a).

This was the sort of power that produced results. This consisted in signs that carried clear meaning, in wonders that produced amazement among the people, and in the Holy Spirit who wrought within them.

3. *Preaching the gospel was the outstanding ingredient of this ministry* (v. 19b). He carried the gospel from Jerusalem through Palestine and Asia Minor and the entire peninsula of Greece. In his estimation this was a full and effective ministry.

4. *Plan may explain why his ministry was so wide and effective* (vv. 20-21). He laid his plans carefully, determined that he would move among those Gentiles where the gospel had never yet been preached. He did not want to build on another man's foundation. More than that, a passage of Scripture from the Old Testament had gripped his heart (Isa. 52:15), and he wanted to be the human instrument for its fulfillment.

C. A purposeful ministry is clearly exhibited in the way Paul writes to this congregation of saints (vv. 22-29).

1. *Providential prevention marked those years after he had laid plans to reach Rome and the West* (vv. 22-24). Time and again he was hindered from realizing the fulfillment of his plans by responsibility in the Eastern Mediterranean. But now that ministry is finished; so his plans are to go as far west as Spain and stop on the way in Rome for fellowship with them.

2. *Personal priority is given to a responsibility he feels is of the Lord toward his own people in Jerusalem* (vv. 25-27). He has gathered up the offering of the Gentile Christians in Macedonia and Achaia to bring to the poor saints in Jerusalem (cf. II Cor. 8 and 9). Since the Jewish saints had shared with the Gentiles the spiritual things of the gospel, Paul felt it only right that Gentile saints should share their material things with these Jewish saints.

3. *Prosperous prospect of his visit to Rome and Spain now lies before him*, for his responsibility to his Jewish brethren is almost

completed (vv. 28-29). He is confident that his journey to Rome will be in the fulness of the blessing of the gospel of Christ. This will mean that he will impart some spiritual blessing to them, and they in turn will communicate like blessing to him.

D. A prayerful ministry is now launched in which Paul encourages these Roman saints to join him (vv. 30-33).

1. *The appeal for prayer that is addressed to these Roman Christians is threefold:* for the sake of the Lord Jesus Christ, for the love of the Spirit, and for me (v. 30). This means that the apostle is fully aware that the accomplishment of his full ministry depends finally on God.

2. *Two perils confront him as he contemplates what lies ahead* (v. 31). One consisted of the malignant opposition of unbelieving Jews. He was not wrong in this (Acts 20:3, 22; 21:11). He also knew of the antipathy of believing Jews who were narrow and bigoted in their attitude toward Gentiles, and he was concerned that the offering he brought would be acceptable (Acts 15:5; 21:20).

3. *The result formed a part of this prayer* (vv. 32-33). He prayed that the mission to Rome would be joy experienced in the center of God's will and mutual refreshment of spirit. Only the God of peace can minister the necessary tranquility of spirit that he seeks and desires for the saints at Rome. In this one chapter four titles have been used of God: "God of patience" (v. 5); "God . . . of consolation" (v. 5); "God of hope" (v. 13); and, at last, "God of peace" (v. 33).

III. PERSONAL CONTRIBUTION AND THE MINISTRY OF SAINTS (16:1-24)

As indicated earlier in this chapter the movement of thought begun in chapter 12 continues. This is marked by the connective in the opening verse of chapter 16. This means that chapter 16 is no mere appendage to the main discussion of the book but is an integral part of the argument and development of the theme. In

178 THE FIRST CHRISTIAN THEOLOGY

the final section of the book (chaps. 12—16), the apostle is unfolding the practical outworking of salvation in the life of the believer. He is exhorting the believer to demonstrate trans- formation in life as measured by the will of God.

This transformation should display itself in individual living (chap. 12), in political alignments (chap. 13), in Christian fellowship (chap. 14), and in personal contribution (chaps. 15—16). Personal contribution ought to follow the pattern of Christ (15:1-13). Personal contribution ought to conform to the performance of Paul (15:14-33). But there is more. Personal contribution ought to consider the preciousness of the saints (16:1-24). In this sense the apostle brings his argument home to the saints in Rome.

Chapter 16 then becomes more than a mere recitation of names and a collection of greetings and salutations. It is the calling of the roll of a large portion of the membership in the church at Rome and an evaluation on the part of Paul of the personal contribution these saints have made to his own life. They are precious to him for the investment that each has made in his own life. Surely this will result in the kindling of precious memories on the part of those who are named, but in addition it will provide a warmth of affection through which they will be able to see the practical outworking and value of the very thing the apostle is endeavoring to teach.

A. Recognition begins with commendation of Phoebe, a member of the church in Cenchrea (vv. 1-2). She was a deacon- ess in the church and in some sense a woman acting in the capacity of a patroness and guardian over others. She doubtless served in the same capacity as Lydia in Philippi, opening her home to the saints and especially to traveling evangelists like Paul. She was probably the convert of Paul who immediately responded by ministering to his physical needs. Her ministra- tion to him meant so much that in outgoing affection he urges the saints in Rome to receive her and make every effort to assist her in the business she has in Rome. Inasmuch as she is making the journey to Rome, she not only carried this letter but also provided for Paul a bridge of contact with this assembly of saints.

B. From this point the apostle turns to the contributions of the many saints now in Rome who in one way or another had become part of his life in his previous ministry (vv. 3-16). For various reasons these saints had migrated to Rome, the center of the empire. Life in the church is made so authentic. Notice the number of women who are mentioned. Home life in relation to the gospel is depicted. In those days the assemblies of the saints met in homes. The element of service to one another is hallowed. The experience of suffering in behalf of God's people is noted. Paul was often the object of such concern. Varieties of activity are discussed. Some labored strenuously for the gospel, others were associated with great courage, while other Christians were noted for beauty of character. In the midst of this variety, there is an amazing oneness. This was due to the fact that they shared the same life and possessed one object of worship, the Lord Jesus Christ. Honor of these people is so notable. Most of these people are slaves and unknown, but in this community they are saints. Their names are in the book of remembrance (Mal. 3:16, 17). Some are referred to as "beloved," "of note among the apostles," "helpers," "fellowprisoners," "kinsman," "approved," "chosen." Nearly all those mentioned are humble folk, not leaders. In a subordinate, simple, quiet way each made his contribution to the apostle and to the Lord Jesus Christ. All this exhibits in garments of splendor the fellowship of the saints.[4]

> Blest be the tie that binds
> Our hearts in Christian love;
> The fellowship of kindred minds
> Is like to that above.

C. Paul now gives consideration to the spiritual welfare of the church (vv. 17-21). Wherever the blessings of God have come to

4. Thomas, *The Devotional Commentary: Romans Vol. III.* pp. 154-61.

dwell, into that assembly Satan is bound to plant tares to disturb and distress and destroy. Those members live contrary to the doctrine. They are not devoted to Christ. They deceive with fair speeches. And they are given to low and sensual behavior. So Paul urges the saints to be on their guard, to be wise in their conduct, and to be absolutely sincere in their devotion to the Lord. For encouragement he reminds them that the God of peace will eventually bring Satan to his knees and place him under their feet. Grace will carry them through to that day of triumph.

D. The conclusion consists of a whole round of further salutation and greetings (vv. 22-24). Since Tertius is taking down this letter for Paul, his own salutation is included. Gaius, Erastus, Quartus, and the whole church in Corinth are also included in these greetings. Once more, that word most precious since that day on the Damascus road, "grace," Paul leaves with them.

As a formal and final conclusion to the entire epistle a benediction follows that compresses into a few words the message of the entire epistle (vv. 25-27). It is at once a summary of the epistle, a supplication in behalf of the saints at Rome, and a doxology addressed to God. Paul has done his utmost by letter to provide a message that will establish the saints in the faith. Now he commits these dear ones to the power of God. In this final moment we see Paul looking upward. "To God only wise, be glory through Jesus Christ for ever. Amen."

Questions for Individual Study

1. Is there any indication from the material and movement of thought in chapters 15 and 16 that these chapters belong to the epistle and are in their proper place?
2. What is the main theme of these two chapters in relation to the final section (chaps. 12—16) of the book?
3. What two qualities did Christ display in His ministry of service to others?
4. What is meant by the reference to Christ as a minister of the circumcision?
5. How did the ministry of the apostle Paul provide an example for personal contribution on the part of the saints?

6. What purpose does chapter 16 serve in developing the theme of the final two chapters of the epistle?

7. What are some of the contributions made by saints known to Paul as set forth in this chapter?

Bibliography

I. LIFE OF THE APOSTLE PAUL

Barnes, Albert. *The Life of the Apostle Paul*. Grand Rapids: Baker Book House, 1950.

Burton, Ernest Dewitt. *A Handbook of the Life of the Apostle Paul*. Chicago: The University of Chicago Press, 1917.

Deissmann, Adolf. *St. Paul, A Study in Social and Religious History*. New York: Hodder and Stoughton, 1912.

Garvie, Alfred E. *Studies of Paul and His Gospel*. Cincinnati: Jennings and Graham, 1911.

Jones, Maurice. *St. Paul the Orator*. London: Hodder and Stoughton, 1910.

Lineberger, Lawrence O. *The Man from Tarsus*. New York: Fleming H. Revell Co., 1933.

Longenecker, Richard N. *Paul, Apostle of Liberty*. New York: Harper and Row, 1964.

Macartney, Clarence E. *Paul the Man*. London: Williams and Norgate, Ltd., 1929.

Ramsay, William M. *Pauline and Other Studies*. Grand Rapids: Baker Book House, 1970.

_____. *St. Paul the Traveller and the Roman Citizen*. New York: G. P. Putnam's Sons, 1908.

_____. *The Cities of St. Paul*. New York: Hodder and Stoughton, 1907.

Ridderbos, H. N. *Paul and Jesus*. Philadelphia: The Presbyterian and Reformed Publishing Co., 1958.

Robertson, A. T. *Epochs in the Life of Paul*. New York: Charles Scribner's Sons, 1909.

Sabatier, Auguste. *The Apostle Paul*. London: Hodder and Stoughton, n.d.

Sell, Henry T. *Bible Studies in the Life of Paul*. New York: Fleming H. Revell Co., 1904.

Speer, Robert E. *The Man Paul*. New York: Fleming H. Revell Co., 1900.

Stalker, James. *The Life of St. Paul*. New York: Fleming H. Revell Co., n.d.

Whyte, Alexander. *Saul Called Paul*. Grand Rapids: Zondervan Publishing House, 1955.

II. INTRODUCTION TO THE EPISTLE OF ROMANS

Guthrie, Donald. *New Testament Introduction: The Pauline Epistles*. Chicago: The Inter-Varsity Press, 1964.

Harrison, Everett F. *Introduction to the New Testament*. Grand Rapids: Wm. B. Eerdmans Publishing Co., 1964.

Hayes, D. A. *Paul and His Epistles*. Grand Rapids: Baker Book House, 1969.

Hiebert, D. Edmond. *An Introduction to the Pauline Epistles*. Chicago: Moody Press, 1974.

Tenney, Merrill C. *The New Testament*. Grand Rapids: Wm. B. Eerdmans Publishing Co., 1953.

Thiessen, Henry Clarence. *Introduction to the New Testament*. Grand Rapids: Wm. B. Eerdmans Publishing Co., 1943.

Unger, Merrill F. *Bible Handbook*. Chicago: Moody Press, 1966.

III. COMMENTARIES ON THE EPISTLE TO ROMANS

Alford, Henry. *The Greek Testament, Vol. I: Romans*. London: Rivingtons, 1855.

Allen, Leslie C. *A New Testament Commentary*. Grand Rapids: Zondervan Publishing House, 1969.

Arnold and Ford. *An American Commentary on the New Testament: Romans*. Philadelphia: American Baptist Publication Society, 1889.

Barnes, Albert. *Epistle to the Romans*. New York: Harper and Brothers, 1862.

Barnhouse, Donald Grey. *Exposition of Romans*, 10 Vols. Grand Rapids: Wm. B. Eerdmans Publishing Co., 1964.

Beet, J. Agar. *St. Paul's Epistle to the Romans*. London: Hodder and Stoughton, 1900.

Bruce, F. F. *The Epistle to the Romans*. Grand Rapids: Wm. B. Eerdmans Publishing Co., 1969.

Calvin, John. *Epistle to the Romans*. Grand Rapids: Wm. B. Eerdmans Publishing Co., 1947.

Chalmers, Thomas. *Epistle of Paul to the Romans.* New York: Robert Carter, 1843.

Clark, Gordon H. *The Biblical Expositor: Romans, Vol. III.* Philadelphia: A. J. Holman Co., 1960.

DeHaan, Richard W. *The World on Trial.* Grand Rapids: Zondervan Publishing House, 1973.

Denney, James. *Expositor's Greek Testament, Vol. II: Romans.* New York: George H. Doran Co., n.d.

Findlay, G. G. *The Epistles of Paul the Apostle.* New York: Wilbur B. Ketcham, n.d.

Gifford, E.H. *Bible Commentary, Vol. III: Romans.* New York: Charles Scribner's Sons, 1907.

Godet, F. *Epistle to the Romans.* New York: Funk and Wagnalls, 1883.

Gore, Charles. *Epistle to the Romans,* 2 Vols. London: John Murray, 1900.

Haldeman, I. M. *The Branches of the Olive Tree.* New York: Haldeman, n.d.

Harrison, Norman B. *His Salvation: Romans.* Chicago: Bible Institute Colportage Association, 1926.

Hodge, Charles. *Epistle to the Romans.* Philadelphia: James S. Claxton, 1866.

Johnson, Alan F. *The Freedom Letter.* Chicago: Moody Press, 1974.

Lange, J. P. *Lange's Commentary: Romans.* New York: Charles Scribner's Sons, 1915.

Lard, Moses E. *Paul's Letter to the Romans.* St. Louis, Mo.: John Burns Publishing Co., 1875.

Laurin, Roy L. *Romans: Where Life Begins.* Wheaton: Van Kampen Press, 1954.

Lenski, R. C. H. *St. Paul's Epistle to the Romans.* Columbus: Wartburg Press, 1945.

Liddon, H. P. *Epistle to the Romans.* London: Hodder and Stoughton, 1900.

Lloyd-Jones, D. Martyn. *Romans: Atonement and Justification.* Grand Rapids: Wm. B. Eerdmans Publishing Co., 1970.

_____. *Romans: The New Man.* Grand Rapids: Wm. B. Eerdmans Publishing Co., 1973.

_____. *Romans: The Law: Its Functions and Limits*. Grand Rapids: Wm. B. Eerdmans Publishing Co., 1974.

MacDuff, J. R. *Practical Exposition of Chapter VIII*. London: James Nisbet and Co., 1891.

McClain, Alva J. *Romans, The Gospel of God's Grace*. Chicago: Moody Press, 1973.

_____. *Epistle to the Romans, Outlined and Summarized*. Winona Lake, Ind.: The Brethren Missionary Herald Co., 1971.

_____. *The Jewish Problem and Its Divine Solution*. Winona Lake, Ind.: Brethren Missionary Herald Co., 1944.

McGee, J. Vernon. *Reasoning Through Romans*, 2 Vols. Pasadena, Calif.: Thru The Bible Books, 1973.

Mauro, Philip. *God's Gospel and God's Righteousness*. New York: Gospel Publishing House, n.d.

Meyer, Heinrich August W. *Epistle to the Romans*. New York: Funk and Wagnalls, 1884.

Moorehead, William G. *Outline Studies in the New Testament: Acts to Ephesians*. Pittsburgh: United Presbyterian Board of Publications, 1902.

Morgan, G. Campbell. *Living Messages of the Books of the Bible: Matthew to Revelation*. New York: Fleming H. Revell Co., 1912.

_____. *An Exposition of the Whole Bible*. New York: Fleming H. Revell Co., 1959.

_____. *The Analyzed Bible: Romans*. London: Hodder and Stoughton, 1909.

Morison, James. *Critical Exposition of Romans Chapter III*. London: Hamilton, Adams, and Co., 1866.

_____. *Exposition of Romans Chapters 9 and 10*. London: Hodder and Stoughton, 1888.

Moule, H. C. G. *Cambridge Bible: Romans*. Cambridge: University Press, 1903.

Murray, John. *Epistle to the Romans*. Grand Rapids: Wm. B. Eerdmans Publishing Co., 1973.

Newell, W. R. *Romans*. Chicago: Grace Publications, 1938.

Pettingill, William L. *Simple Studies in Romans*. Harrisburg, Pa.: Fred Kelker, 1915.

Phillips, John. *Exploring Romans.* Chicago: Moody Press, 1972.

Plummer, Wm. S. *Commentary on Romans.* Grand Rapids: Kregel Publications, 1971.

Robertson, A. T. *Word Pictures in the New Testament: Vol. IV. Romans.* New York: Richard R. Smith, Inc., 1931.

Sanday, W. and Headlam. *International Critical Commentary: Romans.* New York: Charles Scribner's Sons, 1906.

Sanday, W. *The Handy Commentary: Romans.* London: Cassell and Co., n.d.

Shedd, W. G. T. *Epistle of St. Paul to the Romans.* New York: Charles Scribner's Sons, 1879.

Stuart, Moses. *Epistle to the Romans.* Andover, N.Y.: Gould and Newman, 1835.

Tholuck, Fred. A. G. *St. Paul's Epistle to the Romans.* Philadelphia: Sorin and Bell, 1844.

Thomas, W. H. Griffith. *The Devotional Commentary: Romans,* 3 Vols. London: The Religious Tract Society, n.d.

Tucker, W. Leon. *Studies in Romans.* New York: Charles C. Cook, 1915.

Vincent, Marvin R. *Word Studies in the New Testament, Vol. III: Romans.* New York: Charles Scribner's Sons, 1901.

Wuest, Kenneth S. *Romans in the Greek New Testament.* Grand Rapids: Wm. B. Eerdmans Publishing Co., 1970.